Public Services Inspection in the UK

RESEARCH HIGHLIGHTS 50

Research Highlights in Social Work

This topical series examines areas of particular interest to those in social and community work and related fields. Each book draws together different aspects of the subject, highlighting relevant research and drawing out implications for policy and practice. The project is under the editorial direction of Professor Joyce Lishman, Head of the School of Applied Social Studies at the Robert Gordon University in Aberdeen, Scotland.

Public Services Inspection in the UK

Edited by
Howard Davis
and Steve Martin

RESEARCH HIGHLIGHTS 50

Jessica Kingsley Publishers
London and Philadelphia

MT

Acknowledgements

We acknowledge with gratitude the editorial board of the Research Highlights series and the series editor Professor Joyce Lishman for asking us to put together this analysis of the development and operation of public services inspection in the UK.

We are grateful to the colleagues who agreed to contribute chapters. We wish to thank Stephen Jones and his team at Jessica Kingsley Publishers for their encouragement and guidance. We thank our families for their love and support.

Howard Davisand Steve Martin, March 2008

First published in the United Kingdom in 2008 by
Jessica Kingsley Publishers
116 Pentonville Road
London N1 9JB, UK
and
400 Market Street, Suite 400
Philadelphia, PA 19106, USA

www.jkp.com

Library of Congress Cataloging in Publication Data

Public services inspection in the UK / edited by Howard Davis and Steve Martin.
p. cm. -- (Research highlights in social work ; 50)
ISBN 978-1-84310-527-5 (alk. paper)
1. Municipal services--Great Britain--Evaluation. 2. County services--Great Britain--Evaluation. 3. Inspection--Great Britain. 4. Local government--Great Britain. I. Davis, Howard. II. Martin, Steve, 1960-
HD4645.A5P83 2008
352.8'82140941--dc22

2008006547

British Library Cataloguing in Publication Data
A CIP catalogue record for this book is available from the British Library

ISBN 978 1 84310 527 5

Printed and bound in Great Britain by
Athenaeum Press, Gateshead, Tyne and Wear

5/5/09

Contents

Tables and Figure

CHAPTER 1

The Rise of Public Services Inspection

Steve Martin and Howard Davis

Introduction

External inspection of public services is nothing new. But over the last two decades it has become increasingly important to the point where it has come to play a pivotal role in the management of hospitals, schools, the police, local government and a host of other services. Not surprisingly this has proved controversial. While advocates of inspection see it as a powerful means of improving accountability driving improvement, its detractors argue that it places a huge 'bureaucratic burden' on inspected bodies and diverts resources from 'frontline' service delivery.

But in spite of the lively debate that it has provoked among policymakers and practitioners, the rise of inspection has attracted relatively little academic analysis. This book is designed to help fill the gap by examining the changing nature and role of inspection of UK public services in order to help advance both academic and policy debate about its operation and impacts. It analyses current developments in inspection across a range of key public services, evaluates the benefits and limitations of inspection, and examines the challenges which confront inspectorates across a range of key public services.

Each of the chapters has been specially commissioned and written by experts in the field. Chapters 2 to 6 examine inspection in specific services – local government, social care, the health service, education and skills and the criminal justice system – and each of them covers the same core set of issues. The contributors analyse how inspection arrangements have evolved in their sector.

They describe the current arrangements for inspection, highlighting variations between different parts of the UK. They summarise the available evidence of the impacts of inspection in their sector – their achievements, unintended consequences, and the direct and indirect costs. They highlight key issues for the future development of inspection and for research: How is inspection in each sector likely to change over the next few years? What are the gaps in our current knowledge of inspection in terms of its effects on services, service providers and service users? And what are the implications for future research?

Following these five sector-specific chapters, the book offers two contrasting views of current approaches to public services inspection in the UK. Chapter 7 takes a broadly supportive view of inspection, enumerating what the authors see as its benefits and describing how the inspectorates have been responding to calls for more 'holistic' approaches. Chapter 8 takes a far more critical stance. It questions many of the claims made for inspection, arguing that paradoxes built into the intentions, design and implementation of these performance evaluation systems render them incapable of delivering what they purport to.

In the final chapter we draw together the common themes that emerge from the analyses of the different service settings represented in the book. We then analyse the evidence about the impacts of inspection both on accountability and on performance improvement. In closing we highlight the main challenges that are likely to face inspection in the UK over the coming years.

In this introductory chapter we set the scene for the rest of the book. We first define some key terms and then examine how public services inspection is distinguished from other forms of external regulation. Next we describe alternative approaches to inspection. We then discuss the theories that have influenced current approaches to public services inspection in the UK. In the final section we analyse the recent expansion of inspection and the potential costs and benefits associated with this.

Approaches to inspection

As Jane Martin notes in Chapter 4, the origins of public service inspection in the UK date back at least as far as the early nineteenth century (see also Davis, Downe and Martin 2001). However, the context within which it now takes place is fundamentally different from the one in which it operated 200 years ago. Then services were provided by local organisations that were for the most part independent of the central state. There were few central oversight mechanisms. There was little by way of any universal entitlement to welfare provision, and public expectations of services were of course entirely different.

Inspection is, of course, only one of the mechanisms by which the public and politicians hold public service providers to account. Hood, James and Scott (2000) identify five distinct forms of what they call 'regulation inside government': audit, inspection, adjudication, authorisation and certification. They describe an array of regulatory methods including the enforcement of legal requirements; the use of financial incentives to modify behaviour; the dissemination of good practice; and the publication of performance ratings. While regulation is often seen as restricting what inspected bodies are able to do (for example, rules constraining local councils' powers to trade), it can also be enabling (for example, the power to promote well-being that was granted to local authorities in England and Wales in the Local Government Act 2000) or mandatory (for example, the duty to collaborate placed on local agencies in Scotland by the 2003 Local Government Act).

Some commentators define regulation much more narrowly than Hood and his colleagues. The independent review of the regulation of public services in Scotland, undertaken in 2007, defined it as 'a licence to operate' or 'the means by which standards that were set for entry into a market' (Scottish Government 2007). It saw regulation as one of four forms of 'external scrutiny', with the other three being audit, inspection and complaints systems. Some other observers have, however, conflated one or more of these activities. Power (1994, 1997), for example, uses the phrases 'audit society' and 'audit explosion' to describe the growth in financial audit, inspection and other forms of scrutiny. Similarly, writing in Chapter 8 of this book, John Clarke uses the term 'evaluation' as a catch-all covering audit, inspection and scrutiny of public services.

Most authors define 'audit' more narrowly than Power, seeing it as the process of providing assurance about the financial viability and probity of public bodies through regular (often annual) checks of an organisation's accounts and financial management systems. By contrast inspection has traditionally been seen as concerned with service quality and outcomes and drawing upon quality assurance methods. It usually entails selective, episodic checks that organisations are meeting their obligations as defined by law or according to professional norms and best practice. In contrast to auditors, inspectors usually have specialist professional knowledge and direct operational experience of running the services that they are scrutinising.

In recent years, however, the boundary between audit and inspection has become blurred (Davis, Downe and Martin 2004). The rise of performance and value-for-money auditing has meant that auditors have taken an increasing interest in performance management systems and corporate governance (Pollitt 2003; Public Audit Forum 2002). The result has been what Power (2003, p.189) describes as a 'homogenization and standardization of audit and inspection processes in terms of focusing on systems'. Inspectors and auditors have begun to 'blend their respective concerns with quality and efficiency' (Midwinter and McGarvey 2001, p.843).

Most definitions of public services inspection differentiate between what might be called 'hard-edged' and more 'consensual' approaches. Hughes, Mears and Winch (1997) contrast 'non-punitive' approaches based on peer review and controlled by professions with what they describe as 'punitive' approaches which are imposed by central government and based on managerialist frameworks. McGarvey and Stoker (1999) use a similar typology. They differentiate between 'collegial/emancipatory' approaches which emphasise self-responsibility, self-evaluation and self-regulation and what they call 'bureaucratic/technicist' which are based on rules, procedures, accountability, compliance and sanctions. Similarly, Day and Klein (1990) identify 'consultancy'-based approaches which rely on techniques of persuasion and compare these to 'policing' approaches which rely on enforcing rules.

The differences between 'hard-edged' and more consensual approaches to inspection are often explained in terms of the 'relational distance' between the inspectors and those whom they are inspecting. Hood *et al.* (1999) suggest: 'The more distant such regulators were from their "clients" in professional-social backgrounds, the more regulatory they tended to be in the sense of more formal and more rule-bound.' They contrast police and fire inspectorates, which are close to the bodies that they inspect and favour persuasion rather than sanctions, with the work of the Audit Commission, which according to Hood *et al.* is more detached from inspected bodies and more inclined to impose sanctions on them. Hughes *et al.* (1997) believe that the public standing of inspected bodies, the kinds of knowledge and expertise they lay claim to and the extent to which members of a profession present a united front are important additional determinants of the nature of inspection processes.

Several of the chapters in this book chart the way in which over the last two decades public services inspection has increasingly embraced more 'hard-edged', managerialist approaches. This theme is also noted by several other authors. Hughes *et al.* (1997), for example, claim that 'OFSTED has become a body which belongs very much at the policing end of the continuum of activities of inspection, particularly as they have recently taken on the task of reporting on the effectiveness of individual teachers.' Similarly, Day and Klein (1990) describe how the Social Services Inspectorate (SSI) abandoned the 'professional-consultancy' approach developed by its predecessor the DHSS's Social Work Service in favour of an increasing focus on performance improvement and good management practice, a move which precipitated what Henkel (1991) describes as a conflict between the 'humanitarian' and professional values and the pursuit of economy, efficiency and effectiveness. In Chapter 3 of this volume Johns and Lock update this analysis, describing the recent development of inspection in social care. Police inspection has followed a similar path. As Carter, Day and Klein (1992) note: 'After 1983 inspection became a more serious affair in which the inspectors helped set objectives, assessed their achievement, and had the duty of examining financial information.' (See also Reiner 1991.) The story of inspection of policing is described in more detail by John Raine in Chapter 6.

Theories of inspection

The typologies discussed above are a useful means of identifying differences between inspectorates and changes that are taking place in inspection methodologies. But to understand what drives the developments analysed in subsequent chapters of this book it is necessary to look at the theories which have influenced and informed inspection. These have for the most part been implicit rather than explicit. Neither the government nor the local inspectorates have rushed to spell out the thinking that underpins inspection methodologies. But there are at least three broad theories or models of inspection that can be identified in current policy discourse (Grace 2005).

The first is a fairly traditional model that sees the primary role of inspection as being to provide an independent check on public service providers and in some cases to advise government on future policy direction. This approach focuses on providing assurance, and according to Grace (2005) sees inspection as in effect part of a 'fourth arm of governance' which operates alongside the executive, the legislature and the judiciary.

A second and increasingly influential view of inspection is that as well as providing assurance it must 'drive' improvement (Kelly 2003). Until 10 or 15 years ago public services were judged primarily in terms of whether they met minimum standards, which were usually established by either statute and/or agreed standards of professional 'good practice'. In recent years most public service providers have been given a statutory duty to achieve continuous improvement. The English Local Government Act 2000, for example, requires local councils, police and national park authorities to 'make arrangements to secure continuous improvement in the way functions are exercised' (HMSO 1999, clause 3.1; see Chapter 2) and the Local Government Act 2003 placed a similar statutory duty on councils in Scotland. Inspectors are now therefore expected not just to check that services are meeting minimum standards but that they are also improving over time and to provide a stimulus for them to do so. This still relatively new 'assurance and improvement' paradigm is reflected in a host of government reports and policy statements. The Cabinet Office White Paper *Modernising Government* states: 'Inspection has a positive role to play in supporting improvements in services as well as in providing assurance about standards' (Cabinet Office 1999, p.46). The Treasury's review of the role of inspection undertaken by Sir Ian Byatt and Sir Michael Lyons (who went on to hold a senior position in the Audit Commission) argued that it must support the leaders of local service providers 'in effecting change' (Byatt and Lyons 2001, p.4). The policy statement *Inspecting for Improvement*, published by the Prime Minister's Office, stated: 'Inspection has a key role to play in the reform and improvement of public services' (OPSR 2003, p.i). 'Checking compliance with rules and regulations' has, it says, 'been superseded by today's needs for inspection to be a catalyst for better local leadership, confidence, creativity and innovation' (OPSR 2003, p.2). Scotland's Auditor General, Bob Black, has stated that as well as aiding democratic scrutiny 'public audit should also be providing high quality risk-based reports and advice to public organisations to challenge and assist them in improving their performance' (Black 2004, p.6).

A third view of inspection sees it as a surrogate for the competitive pressures that private businesses face, but which public services are largely insulated from because users of public services usually do not pay for them directly or opt out of services which fall short of their expectations. According to this view, the purpose of inspection is to exert external pressure to drive down costs and drive up service quality, in a similar fashion to the way in which regulators of privatised utilities, such as Ofwat, Ofcom and Ofgem, operate. To date this theory of inspection has had less influence than the 'assurance and improvement' paradigm described above. But it is being espoused by senior figures in several of the key inspectorates. The chief executive of the Audit Commission, for example, has argued that inspectors need to 'develop a more active market management role' which could involve 'promoting mergers and acquisitions among private or voluntary sector providers or actively encouraging new entrants to the market for public service provision'. He suggests that inspectorates should increasingly 'mirror the regulation of monopolies in the private sector by playing a role in price fixing or in the prescription of compulsory activities' (Bundred 2005, p.60). James Strachan, the former chair of the Audit Commission, took a similar line, stating that 'the regulator's challenge has been to create a substitute form of pressure' (quoted in Grace 2005, p.588). The then Chair of the Commission for Social Care Inspection, which inspected private care homes and local authority provision, defined its role as regulating the market for social care of adults (Platt 2005). Not surprisingly given this high-level support, this view of inspection is manifested in a range of recent policies including in particular the work of the 'Better Regulation Executive' created in 2005 by the Treasury to oversee regulation in both the public and private sectors.

The three theories of inspection are not, of course, mutually exclusive, but they do imply rather different approaches. An assurance-based model will be concerned primarily with checking that minimum standards and professional good practice are being met. An 'inspection for improvement' paradigm will focus primarily on managerial competence. A regulation-based approach will be concerned to create the conditions under which markets can operate in ways in which service users can make choices between alternative providers. The increasing emergence of the 'assurance and inspection' model of inspection in different sectors is explored in more detail in Chapters 2 to 6 and is an issue to which we return in our conclusions in Chapter 9.

The expansion of inspection

One of the themes that runs right through the rest of this book is the extraordinarily rapid expansion in the scale, scope and intensity of inspection of public services which has taken place in the UK over the last 30 years. Hood *et al.* (1999) found that between 1976 and 1995 the number of arm's length regulators of government in the UK increased by more than a fifth; spending on regulation more than doubled; the staff employed by regulators grew by at least 90 per cent. The pace and scale of change have been even more breathtaking under New Labour (Davis *et al.* 2001, 2004). The first five years of the Blair government saw the creation of a new Benefit Fraud Inspectorate (BFI) in 1997; the Trading Standards Council and the Youth Justice Board in 1998; the Best Value inspectorate, the General Teaching Council for England, Wales and NI and HM Crown Prosecution Service Inspectorate in 2000; and the Standards Board for England in 2001. As Walshe shows in Chapter 5, managerialist inspection frameworks have had an increasing impact even upon the powerful and traditionally highly regarded medical profession. As several of the other chapters in this volume demonstrate, while other parts of the UK have been less wedded to the use of targets and published league tables (Bevan and Hood 2006), the growth of inspection is far from being an exclusively English phenomenon. At least ten new public service inspectorates were created in Scotland in the seven years between 1999 and 2006 (Scottish Government 2007), and similar developments have been witnessed in Wales and Northern Ireland.

As several of the chapters in this book also show, one of the results of this expansion in inspection has been that many public services have been subjected to rigorous external scrutiny for the first time. Ofsted has for example taken on the inspection of government funded nursery schools. The creation of the BFI and the new duty of 'Best Value' meant that a host of additional local government services – including housing, environmental services, planning, culture and leisure – became subject to inspection. Right across the public sector, inspection reports have become more influential than they were in the past. Inspectors' judgements now trigger intervention in poor performers and can bring down the careers of head teachers, chief constables and chief executives.

As Downe describes in Chapter 2, the focus of inspection has also increasingly moved 'upwards' from the scrutiny of individual services to assessments of an organisation's corporate capacity and leadership. Comprehensive Performance Assessments (CPAs) in English local government, the Best Value Audit process in Scotland and the Wales Programme for Improvement all emphasise the importance of 'corporate capacity'. In 2007 the Audit Commission announced plans to extend this approach to other organisations with the introduction from 2008/09 of 'Comprehensive Area Assessments' which evaluate the quality of life and the nature of joint working between local agencies in an area (Audit Commission 2007). This regime brings into sharp focus the challenges associated with partnership working and more 'holistic' forms of inspection; a theme which is explored in detail by Bundred and Grace in Chapter 7.

There have been a number of drivers of this growth of inspection in the UK. Several chapters, including Clarke's analysis in Chapter 8, highlight the loss of faith (by national politicians and to a lesser extent by the public) in traditional forms of bureaucratic and professional control as an important factor. Some of our contributors also point to the importance of the 'hollowing out of the state', whereby functions have been hived off to newly created agencies and appointed bodies. This has led the UK government to seek to exercise control through what Hoggett (1996) calls the 'long distant mechanics' of audit and inspection. A third important factor has been that ministers have wanted to ensure that unprecedented levels of real terms increases in public spending in the early part of the current decade result in improvements. They have seen inspection both as a means of encouraging changes that are designed to produce better GCSE exam results, shorter hospital waiting times, increased rates of crime detection, and so forth, and also as a source of 'independent' evidence that the added investment has produced tangible benefits.

As several chapters explain, the increase in inspection has, however, been costly. Between 1998 and 2003 the direct costs of public services inspection in England more than doubled from £250 million to £550 million (OPSR 2003). The costs of running the Office for Standards in Education (Ofsted) increased from £88 million to £201 million and the (then) Social Services Inspectorate doubled its spending from £6 million to £11 million. The cost of Audit Commission inspection increased more than tenfold from just £4 million to more than £50 million, and its workforce increased by almost 90 per cent between 1997 and 2003. By 2005 the direct cost of inspection of local government alone amounted to £97 million per annum (ODPM/HM Treasury 2005). The direct costs of public services inspection in Scotland totalled more than £90 million by the same date (Scottish Government 2007). In addition, of course, inspected bodies incurred a wide range of costs including staff time devoted to preparing for and managing inspection visits.

The government at first turned a 'blind eye' to the mounting concerns about the cost of inspection and the administrative burdens that it placed on schools, NHS trusts, police services, councils and other local service providers. But from around 2004 onwards inspectorates came under pressure to reduce their running costs and co-ordinate their hitherto largely separate activities. They responded with promises of more 'proportionate' or 'risk based' approaches and in 2005 the government published plans to merge a number of local inspectorates. The progress of and prospects for these proposals are explored in more detail in several chapters (notably John Raine's analysis in Chapter 6 of the inspection of the criminal justice system where the proposed mergers did not proceed because of opposition from a range of powerful stakeholders). We also return to this theme in the final chapter.

The impacts of inspection

While it is very clear that the costs of inspection have risen dramatically over the last decade, there is far less certainty about whether and if so it has encouraged improvement in public services. Understandably, many policymakers see this as the 'acid test' of inspection and yet, as the contributions to this book make clear, there is very little robust empirical evidence to inform a cost–benefit analysis of inspection.

Assessing impacts is difficult because, as a range of writers has pointed out, performance is multidimensional (Boyne 2003) and isolating the impacts of inspection from the effects of other factors, such as increases in public spending, the adoption of new technologies or socio-economic factors such as levels of deprivation, is virtually impossible (Andrews 2004; McLean, Haubrich and Gutierrez-Romero 2007). Inspection agencies have insisted that their activities have encouraged improvement, but John Clarke (see Chapter 8) questions the basis of these claims. As Downe points out in Chapter 2, senior local government officers believe that inspection has led to improvements in their services, and there is evidence from Scotland that inspection has had a positive impact on the worst performing councils. However, as Swann *et al.* (2005) note, while the 'floor' has been raised, inspection has not on the whole led to truly transformational changes, and public satisfaction with councils' overall performance has declined. It is conceivable that some of the improvement in

CPA and other inspection scores is therefore because inspected bodies have become much more adept at 'ticking the right boxes' (Downe and Martin 2007). Debates about the impacts, costs and benefits of public services inspection and the implications for the role which it plays in the future are key questions that are addressed in a variety of ways in the contributions to this book, and they are issues to which we return in the final chapter.

References

Andrews, R. (2004) 'Analysing deprivation and local authority performance: The implications for CPA.' *Public Money and Management 24*, 1, 19–26.

Audit Commission (2007) *The Transition from CPA to CAA*. London: Audit Commission.

Bevan, G. and Hood, C. (2006) 'What's measured is what matters: Targets and gaming in the english public health care system.' *Public Administration 84*, 3, 517–538.

Black, B. (2004) *Holding to Account and Helping to Improve*. Audit Scotland: Edinburgh.

Boyne, G.A. (2003) 'What is public service improvement?' *Public Administration 81*, 2, 211–227.

Bundred, S. (2005) 'Regulating Reformed Services.' In M. Bichard and C. Grace (eds) *Perspectives on the Third Term: The Way Ahead*. London: Solace Foundation Imprint.

Byatt, I. and Lyons, M. (2001) *The Role of External Review in Improving Performance*. London: HM Treasury.

Cabinet Office (1999) *Modernising Government, Cmnd 4310*. London: The Stationery Office.

Carter N., Day P. and Klein R. (1992) *How Organisations Measure Success*. London: Routledge.

Davis, H., Downe, J. and Martin, S. (2001) *External Inspection of Local Government: Driving Improvement or Drowning in Detail?* York: York Publishing Services for the Joseph Rowntree Foundation.

Davis, H., Downe, J. and Martin, S. (2004) *The Changing Role of Audit Commission Inspection of Local Government*. York: York Publishing Services for the Joseph Rowntree Foundation.

Day, P. and Klein, R. (1990) *Inspecting the Inspectorates*. York: Joseph Rowntree Foundation.

Downe, J. and Martin, S. J. (2007) 'Regulation inside government: processes and impacts of inspection of local public services.' *Policy and Politics 35*, 2, 215–232.

Grace, C. (2005) 'Change and improvement in audit and inspection: A strategic approach for the 21st century.' *Local Government Studies, 31*, 5, 575–596.

Henkel, M. (1991) *Government, Evaluation and Change*. London: Jessica Kingsley Publishers.

HMSO (1999) *Local Government Act*. London: HMSO.

Hoggett, P. (1996) 'New modes of control in the public service.' *Public Administration 74*, 9–32.

Hood, C., James, O. and Scott, C. (2000) 'Regulation inside government: has it increased, it is increasing, should it be diminished?' *Public Administration 78*, 2, 283–304.

Hood, C., Scott, C., James, O., Jones, G. and Travers, T. (1999) *Regulation Inside Government.* Oxford: Oxford University Press.

Hughes, G., Mears, R. and Winch, C. (1997) 'An inspector calls? Regulation and accountability in three public services.' *Policy and Politics 25,* 3, 299–313.

Kelly, J. (2003) 'The Audit Commission: Guiding, steering and regulating local government.' *Public Administration 81,* 3, 456–476.

McGarvey, N. and Stoker, G. (1999) *Intervention, Inspection, Regulation and Accountability in Local Government.* London: Department of the Environment, Transport and Local Government.

McLean, I., Haubrich, D. and Gutierrez-Romero, R. (2007) 'The perils and pitfalls of performance measurement: The CPA regime for local authorities in England.' *Public Money and Management 27,* 2, 111–118.

Midwinter, A. and McGarvey, N. (2001) 'In search of the regulatory state: Evidence from Scotland.' *Public Administration 79,* 4, 825–849.

Office of the Deputy Prime Minister/HM Treasury (2005) *Securing Better Outcomes: Developing a New Performance Management Framework.* London: ODPM.

Office of Public Services Reform (OPSR, 2003) *Inspecting for Improvement.* London: Cabinet Office.

Platt, D. (2005) 'The Role of Social Care Inspection', Paper presented to the ESRC Seminar Series on: The Development of Scrutiny across the UK. Cardiff: Cardiff University.

Pollitt, C. (2003) 'Performance auditing in western Europe: Trends and choices.' *Critical Perspectives in Accounting 14,* 157–170.

Power, M. (1994) *The Audit Explosion.* London: Demos.

Power, M. (1997) *The Audit Society: Rituals of Verification.* Oxford: Oxford University Press.

Power, M. (2003) 'Evaluating the audit explosion.' *Law and Policy 25,* 3, 185–202.

Public Audit Forum (2002) *The Different Roles of External Audit, Inspection and Regulation.* London: Public Audit Forum.

Reiner, R. (1991) *Chief Constables – Bobbies, Bosses, or Bureaucrats?* Oxford: Oxford University Press.

Scottish Government (2007) *Independent Review of Regulation, Audit, Inspection and Complaints Handling of Public Services in Scotland.* Scottish Government: Edinburgh.

Swann, P., Davis, H., Kelleher, J., Ritters, K., Sullivan, F. and Hobson, M. (2005) *Beyond Competence: Driving Local Government Improvement.* London: Local Government Association.

CHAPTER 2

Inspection of Local Government Services

James Downe

Introduction

This chapter examines the fast-moving landscape of inspection in local government. It begins by providing some historical context of local government inspection before focusing in particular on Best Value and the Comprehensive Performance Assessment (CPA) in England. The different inspection regimes which exist in Scotland (Best Value Audits, BVAs) and Wales (Wales Programme for Improvement, WPI) are introduced and common themes and contrasts with England are discussed. The increasingly central role played by external inspection of local government begs an important question about the extent to which inspection is a driver of service improvement and/or whether the costs involved are outweighed by any performance gains. The final two sections therefore explore the impact of inspection and consider the role it could play in the future.

The history of inspection in local government

Central government has a long history of ensuring that local services are provided at least to a minimum standard. In education, for example, the first two inspectors designated as Her Majesty's Inspectors of Schools were appointed in 1839. However, it was not until the Education (Schools) Act of 1992 that there was a general requirement that all state schools in England and Wales should be inspected on a regular basis by the Office for Standards in Education (Ofsted). The history of inspection of other local government services is much shorter.

In the 1980s and 1990s, the Thatcher and Major administrations aimed to reduce the size and scope of the state and expose local services to market forces through compulsory competitive tendering and other forms of marketisation. This focus on increasing the efficiency of local services alongside the introduction of the Citizen's Charter in 1991, which used targets as a means of public accountability, paved the way for greater inspection in local government, resulting in what Sanderson (2001) describes as an approach which is 'top-down with a dominant concern for enhancing control and upwards accountability' (p.297).

The Audit Commission, which was established in 1983, has played a key role in regulating the provision of local government services. The commission's initial responsibility was to carry out traditional financial and regularity audits, but over time it began to assess the economy, efficiency and effectiveness (the 'three Es') of local authorities through value for money audits. This constituted a very different role for the commission. Rather than simply checking legality and propriety, it was now providing advice on 'issues that go to the heart of the way in which authorities operate' (Radford 1991, p.931). To borrow an analogy that has been used by a number of commentators, including John Clarke in Chapter 7, the 'watchdog' was beginning to act as a 'guide dog'.

In 1992 the Audit Commission was given new powers to specify, collect and publish performance indicators for local authorities, which were intended to provide information to local people about performance (their primary purpose) and allow comparisons between authorities. In 1996 it began to work with inspectorates such as the Social Services Inspectorate (SSI) to jointly review social care, and Ofsted in reviewing local education authorities. The commission also worked with other inspectorates to examine performance in housing and benefit fraud. However, the commission's value for money audits produced only 'partial descriptions, prescriptions and judgements of local authorities' (McSweeney 1988). The introduction of the Best Value regime in England in April 2000 and the CPA, which took effect from December 2002, greatly expanded the coverage of inspection in local government. The next two sections of this chapter describe these important developments in detail.

Best Value

The 1999 Local Government Act required Best Value authorities (local councils and a range of other statutory bodies) to put in place arrangements to achieve continuous improvement, having regard to economy, efficiency and effectiveness in the exercise of their functions. In England and Wales, the guidance initially required authorities to review all of their functions over a five-year period and publish annual statements of current performance, future targets and plans for improvement. Reviews had to respond to the 'four Cs' of the Best Value performance management framework – they had to *challenge* how and why a service was being delivered, *compare* current performance against that of other providers, embrace fair *competition* as a means of securing efficient and effective services, and *consult* with service users, local taxpayers and others with an interest in the service(s) in question (Martin 2001).

The Audit Commission's guide to the way in which it would carry out inspections of Best Value Reviews (BVRs) (Audit Commission 2000) amounted to a declaration of universal inspection of local government services. The commission's intention was to include most of the reviews which authorities undertook in a five-year programme of inspections. It claimed that councils would be able to influence the length and cost of inspections as the nature, intensity and duration of an inspection would 'vary depending on the nature of the services being inspected and, more importantly, on the quality of the authority's own best value review' (Audit Commission 2000, para 18). Where a local authority could demonstrate that it had undertaken a 'comprehensive review', an inspection might be completed in as little as one day. In other cases, inspections might involve a 'full report showing how inspectors' judgements were reached and making recommendation for improvement' and take up to 20 days to complete (Audit Commission 2000, para 19).

There was very little evidence of any flexibility during the first two years of the regime. Instead, the commission seemed to adopt a 'one size fits all' model as inspections followed the same pattern regardless of the nature of the review and the performance of services that were being inspected (Davis, Downe and Martin 2004). Probably the most contentious feature of the regime was that inspection reports rated services' current performance and capacity to improve on a 0 to 3 'star-rating'. Some councils questioned the basis of the scoring system, but the Audit Commission argued that it was an important means of summarising inspection results in a form that would attract the attention of the public and elected members. Increasingly, as the regime bedded in, authorities seemed to accept the system.

Although the commission's budget had nearly doubled between 1998 and 2001 and its staff increased by 60 per cent, it became clear by the summer of 2001, that it did not have the capacity to carry out universal inspection of all BVRs (Martin 2004). Local authorities were conducting far more, and for the most part much more narrowly focused reviews than had been anticipated by the government. In the autumn of 2001 the commission called for a more risk-based approach to Best Value Reviews (BVRs) and to inspection (Audit Commission 2001) and this was affirmed in a new Local Government White Paper (DTLR 2001). The government lifted the requirement for councils to review all of their functions within five years, encouraging them instead to focus on the most important services and those where there was the greatest need for improvement. Councils were told to take a more 'strategic approach' to reviews, focusing on large services and 'cross-cutting' issues rather than what were referred to as traditional service 'silos'.

Comprehensive Performance Assessment

The 2001 White Paper also announced the introduction of Comprehensive Performance Assessment (CPA) in England. The aim of this new form of inspection was to bring together for the first time the key information held by government departments, auditors and inspectors on each council into a single framework. As with Best Value, inspectors made judgements about current performance and the likelihood of future improvements. Judgements about the current performance of authorities were based on audit and inspection reports, statutory performance indicators and assessments by government departments of statutory plans in 'key' services. A council's capacity to improve was based on a self-assessment produced by each authority and an external 'corporate assessment' usually conducted by teams comprising auditors, inspectors, and officers and elected members from 'peer' councils. Each authority was given a score for key blocks of services and an overall score that brought together the assessments of current performance and capacity for improvement. Councils were graded on a five-point scale – 'excellent', 'good', 'fair', 'weak' and 'poor' – and inspection was now closely linked to an improvement plan agreed by an authority and its inspectors. Councils that were judged to be 'excellent' and 'good' were promised that they would be subject to far fewer Best Value inspections than before and would be granted new 'freedoms and flexibilities' to borrow and to trade. Those judged to be 'poor' or 'weak' were to receive more intensive inspection combined with external assistance and support designed to enable them to improve rapidly.

The arrival of CPA had the important effect of shifting local authorities' and regulators' attention away from individual services and focused activities on 'corporate' capacity. This reflected the Audit Commission's view that 'a serious and sustained service failure is also a failure of corporate leadership' (2002, p.19) and its repeated emphasis of the need for good 'corporate performance management'. According to the commission: 'Top performing councils have...sound corporate performance management, commitment to improvement, sustained focus on top local priorities, the ability to shift resources and make difficult choices' (Audit Commission 2002, p.30).

Policy statements issued by the Audit Commission in 2002 and 2003 signalled a key third stage in the development of its approach to the inspection of local government. Acknowledging the concerns about the regime, it stated that 'the current system of regulation of public services is fragmented and there are legitimate concerns about the cost, value and accountability of regulation' which presented 'a significant challenge to regulators' and they 'must be able to demonstrate that the value of their work for audited and inspected bodies and the wider public outweighs the costs' (Audit Commission 2004, p.2).

In the autumn of 2003, the commission laid out the guiding principles of what it called 'strategic regulation'. This involved an approach that sought to concentrate resources where they were most needed and focused on the requirements of all those who use public services. The result would, it said, be a reduction in the overall level of inspection resulting in savings of £18 million in fees to audited and inspected bodies by 2005/2006 with a further £6 million of cost savings to be realised through improved management structures.

Current inspection arrangements for local government in England

CPA rather than the Best Value regime is now the centrepiece of the government's attempts to promote improvement in local government. There has been a shift away from an emphasis on individual services and BVRs which were treated almost in isolation, towards a much greater focus on the improvement of the authority as a whole. This is reflected in particular in the much greater emphasis placed on 'corporate capacity', leadership and authority-wide arrangements for performance management and procurement in the CPA.

The commission has now published CPAs for the 150 single-tier and county councils in England each year since 2002 and CPA has applied to district councils since 2003 and to fire and rescue authorities since 2005. All assessment regimes need to be revised over time to take account of changes in context. In 2004, judgements of partnership working and community leadership were introduced within CPA for the first time and in 2005 a 'harder test' refreshed the original 2002 framework, but placed more emphasis on authorities' performance in addressing local priorities, how they worked in partnership and their use of resources (Audit Commission 2005).

In August 2006, the Audit Commission published proposals for a new performance regime to take effect from 2008 (Audit Commission 2006a). These took account of changes in councils themselves and in the wider context of reform and regulation of public services – in particular the government proposals on the future of public services inspection (ODPM 2005) and the commitment in the 2006 Budget statement to reforming, rationalising and ultimately reducing the overall level of inspection (11 existing inspectorates to be consolidated into four streamlined inspectorates) (HM Treasury 2006). The commission proposed that the post-2008 regime should rely more on local authorities' own performance management and provide area-based assessments, rather than focusing on individual organisations.

These proposals were reflected in the 2006 Local Government White Paper (and the Local Government and Public Involvement in Health Bill) which announced the replacement of CPA from April 2009 with Comprehensive Area Assessments (CAAs) based 'on a combination of risk assessment, largely risk-triggered inspection and audit' (CLG 2006, p.126). While CPA focused on the assessment of council services and corporate processes, the CAA is designed to be more outcome focused. It will not only use the commission's own judgement of services and performance indicators to make a judgement, but also take into account the views of local people, users of services, taxpayers and citizens. The Audit Commission's explicit aim for CAA is to create a new system which is less expensive and intrusive than CPA, but more sophisticated in engaging with users and driving the 'right' kind of service improvement.

Inspection in Scotland and Wales

Best Value Audits in Scotland

A Best Value framework has been in place for Scotland's 32 local councils since 1997, first on a voluntary basis as a quid pro quo for a moratorium on compulsory competitive tendering and from 2003 as a statutory duty (Local Government in Scotland Act). Best Value Audits (BVAs) were introduced by the Accounts Commission in 2004 and 'are designed to give a rounded picture of a council's performance' (Audit Scotland 2006, para 6). The BVAs are 'descriptive rather than prescriptive' as the process starts with a self-assessment which determines the scope of the audit and where resources will be concentrated. BVAs focus on councils' corporate arrangements and make extensive use of information from other inspection reports and statutory performance indicators. The judgement on councils' performance takes local context and scale into account. As a result, no league tables or scores of performance are produced.

The first BVA report was published in 2004 and the aim was to produce reports for all councils over a period of three years. By March 2007, reports on 18 of the 32 councils had been published. Independent research suggests that the BVA approach has gained credibility and, in broad terms, has been effective (Grace *et al.* 2007). Nearly all councils report benefits from the initial process of self-assessment and the systematic review of processes and performance that this has entailed. The greatest overall impact was in those councils that have been judged to have inadequate corporate processes. They have been of limited value in terms of public reporting and there have been low levels of engagement with councils' partners because BVAs have focused on councils' corporate capacity rather than community planning.

The BVA approach has been adapted incrementally, mainly in order to improve evidence-gathering tools and develop sharper and more focused audit reports. The Accounts Commission and Audit Scotland are currently reviewing the BVA approach and in September 2007 an independent review of the scrutiny of public services in Scotland (the Crerar Review, Scottish Government 2007) recommended major changes in the overall arrangements for inspection.

The Wales Programme for Improvement

The Wales Programme for Improvement (WPI) was introduced in 2002 and came fully into effect in 2003/2004. At the outset of the regime, every local authority undertook a whole authority assessment of its capacity to achieve continuous improvement across both corporate and service functions. In the light of this assessment, each council agreed with the Audit Commission a joint risk assessment which then formed the basis of an improvement plan. The risk assessment and the plan are updated regularly and the Wales Audit Office (WAO) produces an annual assessment of the overall progress which is being made. It submits this report on overall progress to a partnership council made up of representatives of the Assembly Government and Welsh local government.

The WPI was developed against the backdrop of a distinctive strategy for public service reforms called 'Making the Connections' which was set out in a key policy statement (WAG 2004) that explicitly rejected the 'English model' of improvement through competition and customer choice and emphasised the need for collaboration – between national and local government, between councils and other local agencies and between neighbouring authorities – to provide more efficient, citizen-centred services (Martin and Webb 2007). This approach was endorsed by an influential review conducted by Sir Jeremy Beecham in 2006 and it is central to the Assembly Government's 2007 local government policy statement (WAG 2007).

Policymakers in Wales believe that performance comparisons are not necessary for improvement and may in fact be counterproductive, demotivating rather than inspiring staff and encouraging gaming by councils. The WPI is therefore unable to generate a standardised score or judgement which can be used to compare performance between authorities. Critics argue that this makes it difficult for the public to know how good services are and means that there is insufficient challenge to poor performance. In its 2007 report on the WPI, the WAO concluded that it provides 'partial assurance that services are improving, but there are weaknesses in its application' (WAO 2007, p.7). An independent analysis of the comparative performance of local public services in Wales and England concluded that 'Policymakers in Wales have developed a distinctive approach to public services delivery, but this has not so far delivered better performance or faster rates of improvement' (Andrews and Martin 2007, p.155).

CPA, BVA and WPI
Common themes and contrasts

There are some significant similarities between CPA, BVA and WPI. All three regimes reflect the importance that has been attached to public service improvement during the last few years and are rooted in the same implicit theory of change which holds that sustained improvement in service outcomes is only achievable where there is effective leadership and robust performance management of the whole council. All three have their roots in a statutory duty on local authorities to secure continuous improvement (as opposed simply to meeting basic minimum standards) and are based on the assumption that professionals cannot be relied on to drive service improvement without an external stimulus to do so (Downe *et al.* 2007).

The most eye-catching difference is in the approach to publishing comparative performance data. While both Scottish and Welsh policymakers have turned their backs on the use of English star ratings to judge an authority's overall performance, there are important differences between their respective approaches. Although there is no overall league table in Scotland, it is clear from BVA reports which make explicit use of Statutory Performance Indicators (SPIs), which authorities are considered to be the top performers. Audit Scotland and the Accounts Commission have also shown themselves willing publicly to name and shame authorities that they believe lack effective leadership and corporate capacity. By contrast, the dearth of performance data in Wales makes it impossible to identity top performers on any systematic basis and the low-key approach to intervention means that failing councils have often gone largely unnoticed by the press or public.

Another key area of difference is in the design and continuing oversight of the three regimes. Although the architects of Best Value inspection and CPA in England had worked in senior positions in local government, the regimes were largely developed by the Audit Commission and central government. Subsequent refinements of the CPA methodology were, of course, informed by discussions with representatives of the local government community, but again they were driven by the commission. CPA is therefore rightly regarded as a 'top-down' regime. By contrast, the WPI and BVA were both developed on a much more consensual basis. A task force involving representatives of the main stakeholders played a key role in the design of the best value criteria in Scotland. In Wales, the WPI emerged from a process of negotiation between local government, central government and the Audit Commission. Subsequent developments and refinements to the approach have been decided on the same tripartite basis.

These differences of approach in part reflect the differences in scale. It is relatively easy for Scottish and Welsh policymakers to consult with and involve 32 and 22 authorities respectively. In-depth consultations with almost 400 councils in England would not be feasible so the Audit Commission has to operate at arm's length. But this is only part of the answer. There is also some evidence that CPA has provided an explicit model to be avoided in Wales because of the strong partnership ethos between the Assembly and local authorities and a strong political aversion to the muscular centralism of local government in England.

The impact of local government inspection

In theory, external review of public services may have a range of benefits. The existence (or threat) of inspection may have a powerful preventative function, encouraging service managers to take greater care than they might have done had external checks not been in place. It can help to ensure that minimum standards are achieved and statutory obligations are fulfilled. By pinpointing failing services, it may help to protect the interests of both service users and taxpayers. To the extent that inspectors are able accurately to diagnose the reasons for failure, they may be able to assist a service to improve and enable others to avoid similar mistakes.

However, inspection is expensive and the direct costs of public service inspection in England have spiralled upwards in recent years (Martin 2005). By 2005, the direct cost of inspecting English local government was in excess of £90 million per annum (ODPM/HM Treasury 2005). There are also significant additional, indirect costs which are borne by inspected bodies but are difficult to quantify (Boyne, Day and Walker 2002; Hood *et al.* 1999; Humphrey 2001). These include the costs of staff time devoted to preparing for, managing and responding to inspections and opportunity costs associated with activities that are foregone as a result of the time taken up by inspection. Hood *et al.* (1998) have estimated that compliance costs at least double the direct costs of inspection.

Given the political importance of service improvement and the time, energy, human capital and public funding being invested in inspection as an agent of improvement, it is surprising that there is 'a continuing "evidence vacuum" about the marginal effects (positive or negative) of increasing or reducing investment in the regulation of government' (Hood, James and Scott 2000, p.298). Boyne concluded from his systematic review of public service improvement that the evidence on the impact of regulatory arrangements is weak and incomplete. He suggested: 'Existing empirical research provides very little basis for conclusions on whether regulatory reforms would lead to service improvement or to deterioration' (2003, p.379).

Theoretical frameworks have been designed that intend to provide a basis for assessing the success of an inspection regime (e.g. Boyne *et al.* 2002) but these have not been tested empirically. Part of the reason for this is that the impact of inspection is difficult to measure. Official statistics from the Audit Commission point to a steady improvement in CPA scores as evidence that the process is encouraging improvement. By 2004, 67 per cent of authorities were rated as 'excellent' or 'good', compared with 51 per cent in 2002. In 2006, under the 'harder test', 79 per cent of single and upper tier authorities were rated as being in the top two performance categories. There is also some evidence from inspection data which suggests that services have improved over the last five years and that inspectors have become increasingly optimistic about the prospects for improvement (Downe and Martin 2007). In social care 'the Commission for Social Care Inspection (CSCI) performance ratings have shown a year-on-year improvement since they were first published in 2002' (CLG 2006, p.116).

There are problems, however, with the commission's evidence base of CPA scores. A number of authors including Jacobs and Goddard (2007) and Cutler and Waine (2003) argue that aggregate measures like CPA scores mask the complex and multifaceted nature of performance and that overall scores are highly sensitive to the weightings which are used. It may be argued that the only improvement that really matters is that experienced by the public and the CPA does not focus enough on this. The Auditor General for Scotland supported this position when he explained in a strategic statement on inspection in Scotland that 'My studies will give greater emphasis to the experience of service users, since this is the key test of whether better services are being delivered' (Audit Scotland 2004, p.4). Unfortunately, the latest best value user satisfaction scores show that, despite the improvement in CPA scores, public satisfaction with the overall performance of English local authorities has fallen by 11 per cent since 2001 (CLG 2007).

Outside of England, research conducted in Wales by Lewis, Phillips and Percy (2007) has concluded that authorities with poor levels of performance have made significant improvements and that external intervention and support is helping councils on their 'improvement journey'. In Scotland, although BVAs have had significant positive impacts on most councils, there is no evidence of a direct impact on service users (Downe *et al.* 2008).

Recent research funded by the Department for Communities and Local Government provides some evidence of officers' perceptions on the impact of inspection. It was suggested earlier that inspection may have a preventative function, it may help to ensure minimum standards and help authorities to improve. In respect of Best Value inspection, only 20 per cent of officers agreed that Best Value inspection ensured that minimum standards of service delivery are achieved and the same proportion of officers believed that inspection would lead to significant improvements in services (Martin *et al.* 2006).

Perceptions on the impact of inspection have not improved over time. In 2004, 44 per cent of officers agreed that the benefits of external inspection outweighed the costs but this figure fell to 28 per cent in 2006. Only one in five officers believed that the regulatory burden of audit and inspection is beginning to reduce in 2006 and less than a third of officers agreed that the activities of the various inspectorates have become more joined up over the previous two years. One aspect of the inspection process that has shown an improvement is the way in which local authorities manage the visits of inspectors. In 2006, 64 per cent of officers agreed with the statement: 'My authority has got better at managing the inspection process in order to get a more positive inspection report.' This is likely to be one of the reasons to explain the aforementioned improvement in inspection scores over time.

The government has recognised that there is room for improvement and that the balance between centrally driven tools and the freedom of local providers to deliver was not quite right (ODPM 2005). As a result, the inspection landscape is changing again in an attempt to reduce costs while ensuring that inspection is focused on areas where it is likely to have the greatest benefit. The new regime will need to be designed in such a way that the Audit Commission and key stakeholders are in a position to conclude whether inspection is a driver of service improvement and if the costs involved are outweighed by any performance gains.

The future of local government inspection

In spite of the lack of clear quantifiable evidence on the impact of external inspection, it is surprising that the rapid growth of local government inspection in recent years has gone largely unchallenged by the local government community. The Audit Commission suggest that CPA has been effective because 'the outcomes were also instantly recognised as legitimate' (Bundred 2007, p.35). Maybe this is why the Local Government Association has focused its efforts on influencing the ways in which the new inspection regimes operate rather than resisting them. For their part, the government and the inspectorates have agreed that, in order to be effective, inspection has to be seen as credible and fair and must be 'owned' by inspected bodies.

There are still a number of challenges for local government inspection. The first is that there needs to be a balance between local diversity and central prescription. Authorities need to develop internal capacity to achieve self-sustaining improvement while also learning from good practice elsewhere. It also means ensuring that 'acceptable' standards of delivery are provided in different parts of the country and the public accepting potentially wide disparities in service standards. The Lyons Inquiry concluded: 'Central and local government should together challenge the presumption that difference between areas – the "postcode lottery" – is always a bad thing' (Lyons 2007, p.13).

The balance between cost savings and improvements in the quality of services is another challenge. Services need to be delivered as cost effectively as possible while also making available the funds needed to invest in long-term improvements in infrastructure and training. Another related issue is the cost effectiveness of inspection itself. Although the Audit Commission has redefined its mission to be a 'strategic regulator' and plan in the medium term to reduce costs by around a third, local authorities in England, Scotland and Wales continue to voice concerns about the cost effectiveness of inspection. They argue that the current scale of inspection activity is still unnecessarily large and out of kilter with what is needed to act as a catalyst for improvement. This is a complaint heard across Europe. In the Netherlands, for example, a review like the Crerar Review in Scotland is being conducted to try and reduce the burden and associated costs of inspection.

A final challenge for local government inspection concerns the impacts of inspection on different stakeholder groups. Internally, it is senior managers who are most involved with inspection, but it is not clear whether the results of inspection cascade down through an authority to front-line staff. Externally, the rhetoric from recent government and Audit Commission statements (Audit Commission 2007; CLG 2007) strongly emphasises the need for more citizen and customer focused inspection. Inspectorates are keen to radically change their approach to ensure that the influence of people who use the services is embedded in the process. Mayo suggests that 'There has never been a time when the role of the consumer in public services has been as central as it is today' (2007, p.21), with different language used in different countries ('choice' in England, 'community' in Wales and 'voice' in Scotland). However, to date there is little evidence of change on the ground. The inspectorates in all three countries are seeking to involve the public to a much greater degree than in the past, but it is not easy to see how they can be involved in overarching inspections such as CPA, BVA and WPI (as opposed to inspection of individual services). There is little doubt that more 'customer' focus and greater public involvement in inspection would be a worthy development, but reaching out and involving the public is going to be difficult to achieve. A recent MORI survey found that 60 per cent of residents disagreed with the statement 'I would like to get involved in helping my council plan and deliver its services' (cited in Ashworth and Skelcher 2005).

The recent Local Government White Paper sets out an agenda for change which addresses some of these challenges by outlining a reduction in national targets and a lighter touch inspection system. The government intends that inspections will be better co-ordinated, more proportionate to risk and make more extensive use of the views of citizens. The Audit Commission will publish an annual Direction of Travel judgement for every local authority which 'will be based on the local authority's track record of improving outcomes, including through its place-shaping role and work with partners, and the progress made in implementing improvement plans' (CLG 2006, p.127).

There has been almost no public debate about alternatives to the inspection process, but there are other approaches. A range of peer review initiatives, 'learning networks' and benchmarking clubs have been in place for some time. Examples include the Local Government Improvement Project ('peer review'; Jones 2005), the Peer Clearing House and the Beacon Scheme run by the IDeA

(Hartley and Downe 2007). The IDeA peer review is viewed very positively by those working in local government. Of authorities which had been reviewed, 88 per cent felt that the scheme was effective in driving through change and 60 per cent suggested that the report had generated more interest within their council than the more formal inspection reports.

Peer review is often seen as a 'softer' alternative to the existing top-down model of control but is more likely to be introduced now that the government has greater confidence in the performance of local authorities. Wales has already gone a long way down the road of self-assessment, and the English Local Government White Paper and the Audit Commission's proposals for CAA signal a growing interest in the potential for regulation from within the local government sector itself. There is a balance to be struck though, as some independent assessment will still be needed to ensure consistency and provide assurance to the public (and government). The Audit Commission's position on this is clear and unsurprising as they argue that 'over-reliance on self-regulation or self-assessment cannot be acceptable' (2006b, p.23).

Central government has accepted that 'Joined-up government requires joined-up regulation to assess the joined-up performance of those joined-up agencies' (Goodship and Cope 2001, p.44). The number of public services inspectorates will be reduced and there will soon be a statutory duty for them to co-operate with each other. This follows the work of the Local Services Inspectorate Forum which has worked with inspectorates to co-ordinate visits to organisations and carried out joint inspections. The Forum reports: 'Since 2001-02, the number of inspection days spent with local councils by local services inspectorates has been reduced by one-third and the number of inspections undertaken reduced by almost fifty per cent' (CLG 2007, p.7).

The increasing recognition of the importance of partnership working presents a considerable challenge for regulators across the UK. The logic of public services reform in all three countries – from local area agreements in England, to the Welsh emphasis on collaboration, to the duty of community planning in Scotland – suggests that CAA, a second round of BVAs and future WPI assessments must focus far more on area-based inspections and much less on individual organisations and sectors. It is clear that this presents formidable challenges and that none of the performance regimes has yet developed a satisfactory solution. The challenge has however been recognised. In England, for example, the government states:

Strong, effective local organisations and local partnerships will be needed to deliver the outcomes that national government and local people want to see. Particular attention will be needed to ensure that local partnerships have the capacity to analyse problems, set robust targets, agree and implement delivery plans and manage performance. (CLG 2006, p.128)

Despite their flaws, the inspection regimes in England, Scotland and Wales have increased self-awareness and encouraged a more corporately focused and outward looking approach. There are also encouraging signs of improvement across local government. There is evidence that the 'shock effect' of inspection, particularly the first round of CPA, has focused authorities' attention on problems that, for whatever reason, they may have previously been unable or unwilling to confront. There were concerns about how such a focus could be sustained as the impact diminishes over time and authorities become better at 'playing the game'. The response to these concerns is the introduction of a 'harder test' which has then been quickly replaced with the CAAs whereby the Audit Commission takes on a wider 'place shaping' perspective to improvement. The future for local government inspection is likely to be 'more of the same' with further changes in the process rather than a fundamental rethink about its purpose and whether an alternative approach to inspection (such as peer review) could have a greater impact.

References

Andrews, R. and Martin, S. J. (2007) 'Has devolution improved public services?' *Public Money and Management 27*, 2, 149–156.

Ashworth, R. and Skelcher, C. (2005) *Progress Report on Accountability in Local Government.* London: ODPM.

Audit Commission (2000) *Seeing is Believing.* London: Audit Commission.

Audit Commission (2001) *Changing Gear: Best Value Annual Statement 2001.* London: Audit Commission.

Audit Commission (2002) *Comprehensive Performance Assessment: Scores and Analysis of Performance for Single Tier and County Councils in England.* London: Audit Commission.

Audit Commission (2004) *Strategic Regulation: Minimising the Burden, Maximising the Impact.* London: Audit Commission.

Audit Commission (2005) *CPA: The Harder Test.* London: Audit Commission.

Audit Commission (2006a) *Assessment of Local Services Beyond 2008.* London: Audit Commission.

Audit Commission (2006b) *The Future of Regulation in the Public Sector.* London: Audit Commission.

Audit Commission (2007) *The Evolution of Regulation: Comprehensive Area Assessment and the Changing Face of Public Service Improvement.* London: Audit Commission.

Audit Scotland (2004) *Holding to Account and Helping to Improve: A Strategic Statement for Public Audit in Scotland 2004–06.* Edinburgh: Audit Scotland.

Audit Scotland (2006) *Annual Report 2005/6: Accountability and Performance.* Edinburgh: Audit Scotland.

Boyne, G. A. (2003) 'Sources of public service improvement: A critical review and research agenda.' *Journal of Public Administration Research and Theory 13*, 3, 367–394.

Boyne, G. A., Day, P. and Walker, R. M. (2002) 'The evaluation of public service inspection: A theoretical framework.' *Urban Studies 39*, 1197–1212.

Bundred, S. (2007) 'CPA in Context – A Brief History of Local Accountability.' In C. Grace (ed.) *Comparing for Improvement.* London: Solace Foundation Imprint.

Communities and Local Government (CLG) (2006) *Strong and Prosperous Communities: The Local Government White Paper.* London: CLG.

Communities and Local Government (CLG) (2007) *Local Services Inspectorate Forum: Delivering a Co-ordinated and Proportionate Approach to Inspection.* London: CLG.

Cutler, T. and Waine, B. (2003) 'Advancing public accountability? The social services "star" ratings.' *Public Money and Management 23*, 125–128.

Davis, H., Downe, J. and Martin, S. J. (2004) *The Changing Role of Audit Commission Inspection of Local Government.* York: Joseph Rowntree Foundation.

Department of Transport, Local Government and the Regions (DTLR) (2001) *Strong Local Leadership, Quality Public Services.* London: The Stationery Office.

Downe, J. and Martin, S. J. (2007) 'Regulation inside government: Processes and impacts of inspection of local public services.' *Policy and Politics 35*, 2, 215–232.

Downe, J., Grace, C., Martin, S. J. and Nutley, S. M. (2007) 'Performance Regimes in England, Scotland and Wales.' In C. Grace (ed.) *Comparing for Improvement.* London: Solace Foundation Imprint.

Downe, J., Grace, C., Martin, S. J. and Nutley, S. M. (2008) 'Best Value Audits in Scotland: Winning without scoring?' *Public Money and Management 27*, 2.

Goodship, J. and Cope, S. (2001) 'Reforming public services by regulation: A partnership approach?' *Public Policy and Administration 16*, 34.

Grace, C., Nutley, S. M., Downe, J. and Martin, S. J. (2007) *Decisive Moment: The Independent Review of the Best Value Audit Process.* Edinburgh: Accounts Commission.

Hartley, J. and Downe, J. (2007) 'The shining lights? Public service awards as an approach to service improvement.' *Public Administration 85*, 2, 329–353.

HM Treasury (2006) *A Strong and Strengthening Economy: Investing in Britain's Future.* London: The Stationery Office.

Hood, C., James, O., Jones, G., Scott, C. and Travers, T. (1998) 'Regulation inside government: Where the new public management meets the audit explosion.' *Public Money and Management 18*, 2, 61–68.

Hood, C., Scott, C., James, O., Jones, G. and Travers, T. (1999) *Regulation Inside Government.* Oxford: Oxford University Press.

Hood, C., James, O. and Scott, C. (2000) 'Regulation of government: Has it increased, is it increasing, should it be diminished.' *Public Administration 78*, 2, 283–304.

Humphrey, J. (2001) 'Bewitched or bewildered? "Facts" and "values" in Audit commission texts.' *Local Government Studies 27*, 2, 19–43.

Jacobs, R. and Goddard, M. (2007) 'How do performance indicators add up? An examination of composite indicators in public services.' *Public Money and Management 27*, 2, 95–102.

Jones, S. (2005) 'Five faults and a submission: The case of the local government improvement programme.' *Local Government Studies 31*, 5, 655–676.

Lewis, M., Phillips, W. and Percy, N. (2007) *Codifying Local Government Support and Intervention*. Cardiff: National Assembly for Wales.

Lyons, M. (2007) *Lyons Inquiry into Local Government: Place-shaping: A Shared Ambition for the Future of Local Government*. London: The Stationery Office.

McSweeney, B. (1988) 'Accounting for the Audit Commission.' *Political Quarterly 59*, 29–43.

Martin, S. J. (2001) 'Implementing Best Value: Local public services in ttransition.' *Public Administration 78*, 1, 209–227.

Martin, S. J. (2004) 'The changing face of public inspection.' *Public Money and Management 24*, 1, 3–5.

Martin, S. J. (2005) 'Evaluation, inspection and the improvement agenda: Contrasting fortunes in an era of evidence based policy making.' *Evaluation 11*, 4, 496–504.

Martin, S. J. and Webb, A. (2007) 'The Conditions for Collaboration: Early Lessons from the Experience of Wales.' In S. Parker and N. Gallagher (eds) *The Collaborative State*. London: Demos.

Martin, S. J., Entwistle, T., Ashworth, R. A., Boyne, G. A., Chen, A., Dowson, L., Enticott, G., Law, J. and Walker, R. M. (2006) *The Long-term Evaluation of the Best Value Regime: Final Report*. London: Department for Communities and Local Government.

Mayo, E. (2007) 'The Road to User-led Public Services.' In C. Grace (ed.) *Comparing for Improvement*. London: Solace Foundation Imprint.

Office of the Deputy Prime Minister (ODPM, 2005) *Inspection Reform: The Future of Local Services Inspection*. London: ODPM.

Office of the Deputy Prime Minister/HM Treasury (2005) *Securing Better Outcomes: Developing a New Performance Management Framework*. London: HM Treasury.

Radford, M. (1991) 'Auditing for change.' *The Modern Law Review 54*, 6, 912–932.

Sanderson, I. (2001) 'Performance management, evaluation and learning in "modern" local government.' *Public Administration 79*, 2, 297–313.

Scottish Government (2007) *The Crerar Review: The Report of the Independent Review of Regulation, Audit, Inspection and Complaints Handling of Public Services in Scotland*. Edinburgh: The Scottish Government.

Welsh Assembly Government (WAG, 2004) *Making the Connections: Delivering Better Services for Wales*. Cardiff: WAG.

Welsh Assembly Government (WAG, 2007) *A Shared Responsibility*. Cardiff: WAG.

Welsh Audit Office (WAO, 2007) *Wales Programme for Improvement: Annual Report 2005/6*. Cardiff: WAO.

CHAPTER 3

Inspection of Adult and Children's Social Care

Chris Johns and David Lock

Development of a regulatory system for social care

The history of the regulation of care services for children and adults in the UK has been characterised by the influence of periodic major crises as well as ongoing public policy initiatives. The relevant legislation currently covers all establishments providing residential and day care for children, residential, continuing nursing care for adults, the boarding element of children and young people in schools (Children Act 1989, S. 87); some specialist colleges providing education and personal care for young adults (the welfare element normally registered as either schools, children's homes or care homes), home care for both adults and children, specialist residential establishments for people who are recovering from mental illness and substance misuse (Care Standards Act 2000). Agencies providing foster care, adoption and nurses are also registered with the regulatory authority in each of the four countries of the UK.

The first form of regulation of 'care' came through Poor Law legislation in the widest sense of requiring harsh conditions in workhouses to deter the poor from relying on aid, and segregating qualifying groups into able-bodied male, female, children, aged and impotent. The requirement under the Poor Law Amendment Act 1834 for workhouses to be managed by three commissioners accompanied by inspectors can be regarded as an important historical moment. Later amendments in 1848 provided for the removal of children from workhouses, and in 1871 the setting up of local government boards to administer the policy (Smith 1972).

The regulation of early years child care from 1800 has a history in 'minding schools' or 'baby farms' in the nineteenth century (Baldock 2001, p.2). Concerns about child welfare before the First World War were reflected in comments by officials in a 1908 report that 'there is no inspection or control' (Ibid.). Petrie (2003) has reviewed the variety of initiatives to provide play centres: extra-school activities and open play areas during the nineteenth century, concluding that care and education occur together and are a means of social control of children.

Nursing homes were first regulated by the Nursing Homes Registration Act 1927, but this was the beginning of a dual structure between health and social care with later relevant legislation made in 1936 (Public Health Act) and 1963 (Nursing Homes Amendment Act; Ridout 1998). The provision of social care continued through the Poor Law regime, but was brought within the provisions of the National Assistance Act 1948, with Section 37 providing for inspection of residential provision. Section 21 of the legislation also placed a duty on local councils that were welfare authorities (county and county borough) to provide residential care for those people who 'for reasons including illness or any other circumstances, are in need of care and attention that is not otherwise available to them'.

This approach to welfare legislation followed the Beveridge model of service provision from 'cradle to grave', but was also driven by professional values. Although government could 'guarantee access to provisions and a broader equality of treatment…the contribution of professionals in health, education and social services should be facilitated' (Davies 2000, p.297). W. Clarke Hall, an advocate of better and regulated provisions for children, remarked that although voluntary 'rescue' homes were providing a crucially important provision, they could be 'very bad indeed':

> The Home Office…realized this and warned magistrates of the danger of sending children to institutions of which they know nothing; but in spite of this there is no Government inspection of them (though the power to inspect exists). (Clarke Hall 1926, p.50)

The Act he was referring to was the Children Act 1908, with Section 25 conferring the power to inspect. The 1933 Child and Young Person's Act established the Schedule 1 offences against children – cruelty; prostitution; begging; burning; or 'dangerous performances'. Section 53 of this Act permitted a child or young person 'to be detained in such a place and on such conditions as the Secretary of State may direct', reflecting changing public attitudes – in some quarters at least – away from punishment of children in favour of greater support and tolerance. This provision gave rise to what subsequently became known as 'secure accommodation' (and later in the 1980s 'secure care'), as far as possible placing young people outside the prison system. The equivalent legislation in Scotland was the Children and Young Persons Act 1937.

The Act gave the Secretary of State the power to appoint inspectors, but at the effective discretion of the Treasury (Jackson *et al.* 1997). Defining and specifying the nature of regulated custody or care was not an explicit and detailed element of the law and regulations. But this was a feature of the Children Act 1948 which provided powers to make regulations as to the conduct of voluntary homes which encompassed accommodation and equipment, clothing, and medical arrangements (Section 31a); furnishing and provision of information to parents (Section 31b); the number of children who could be accommodated (Section 31c); and the person to be appointed in charge (Section 31d). Changes in management and facilities for religious upbringing were regulated by a further two requirements of this Section (Jackson *et al.* on *Clarke Hall and Morrison* 1977).

A registration and inspection system was established through the Nurseries and Childminders Act 1948; the Boarding-Out Regulations of 1955 was an important step; as well as the inspection of premises where foster children were cared for under the Children Act 1958. The 1963–69 Acts provided for the power of inspection of voluntary homes, and put statutory regulation firmly in place in relation to Children's Services prior to the 1980 and 1989 Children Acts and Schedules of Regulations. The 1989 Act, Section 80(6) requires the inspector to: 'inspect the children there; and make such examination into the state and management of the home or premises and the treatment of the children there as he thinks fit'.

However, the Act provides, particularly through its Schedules, the detail of Regulations – Statement of Purpose; Management; Size; Equipment; etc. – and that balances and channels the power. In this manner the 1989 Act maintained Children's regulation ahead of that of the Adult Care sector, and many of its provisions continue to directly underpin regulation today, or otherwise as incorporated into the Care Standards Act 2000. The development of the regulation of care can be seen in the context of change in fundamental principles of the state in the UK: 'The Welfare state began to evolve into the regulatory state in the 1980s' (Day and Klein 1990, p.4).

However, the practice of regulation was in its infancy and – perhaps more importantly – the carer community was often found to operate on a basis of standards that were a 'far cry' from those required by the inspector, who would seek to measure core components of the care process (Davison 1995, p.354). The baseline was minimally acceptable standards and the detection of shortfalls that constitute abuse or neglect.

In the case of adult services, the powers of the National Assistance Act 1948 and the Nursing Homes legislation provided only pragmatic and inconsistent regulatory practices and provisions. Ridout refers to the 1980s as the 'golden age' for care home proprietors, in that government underpinned care home placements through 100 per cent fees support (Ridout 1998, p.13). The combination of this funding and the ageing population led to the realisation that the sector had become – and would continue to become – a significant player in the delivery of care, led to the Registered Homes Act 1984. This incorporated the Residential Care Home Regulations 1984 and was widely interpreted as powers to ensure the regulator 'had teeth' in relation to the care of adults. Staff carrying out regulation and inspection work were officials of local councils who were social services authorities and often also managed council services for children or adults. This model created tensions with independent providers, particularly as council services were not required to be registered and inspected at this time. Associations representing providers lobbied for change in the way in which regulation was organised. They saw a conflict of interest for councils in discharging their statutory duty when purchasing care from independent providers and setting fee levels. It was also held that some councils preferred to use their own accommodation before that of other providers without offering choice to the service user.

Changes in legislation, regulations or procedures have often been as a response to new policy or the findings of a major enquiry into service failure or abuse. Public enquiries across the UK into services where children or adults have suffered abuse or have died – Ely Hospital (Cardiff) 1968; Nye Bevan Lodge (London Borough of Southwark) 1987; Longcare (Buckinghamshire) 1994; North Wales Children's Enquiry 1996 (Waterhouse 2000) – all led to a review of the existing legislation, the introduction of new regulations or the issuing of new guidance to regulatory authorities. The outcome of the Longcare enquiry together with other significant policy initiatives, particularly the early modernisation steps to reshape social services and reform regulation, and the influence of the Burgner Report 1996 led to new legislation, for example, the Care Standards Act 2000.

Any discussion of the policy processes about regulated health and social care services needs then to balance the rational, intentional dimension of social and public policy with the outcomes associated with public 'scandal' about specific service failures. The subject matter of enquiries contrasted with the purposeful development of legislation, for example, in the 1970s, for children and young people and chronically sick and disabled people. There was an optimism that legislative powers and duties would enable councils to contribute to the welfare of citizens in a positive and preventive way. The tragedies, however, invariably pointed to the 'corruption of care' in hospital and residential settings, both for adults and children (Butler and Drakeford 2003; MacLeod 1999; Pring 2003; Taylor 1998; Wardough and Wilding 1993). A public enquiry in 1988 provided a systematic database of residential care weaknesses and strengths, together with a clearly articulated value base for professionals (Wagner 1988).

Policy developments in the regulation of social care were also to demonstrate a shift in government thinking or comprised a response to a particular issue. An example is the setting up of 'arm's length' inspection units in the former local regulatory authorities (local councils and local health authorities) to demonstrate some independence, particularly where the council/health authority was also a purchaser and provider of these services. In most instances units became accountable to the chief executive rather than the director of social services. This enabled a more transparent approach to the inspection of local council services which were now regulated for the first time under the Registered Homes Act 1984 (as amended 1991), and the Children Act 1989. Another significant initiative was the 'direction on choice' which required local councils to demonstrate equity when offering a place in residential care as between available independent and council provision. The change of direction was at least a tacit recognition of groups representing the interests of users, their advocates and providers of services, although these interest groups themselves continued to express concern about the lack of independence of the new local council arm's length 'inspection units'.

In a study of the developing pattern of care regulation Day, Klein and Redmayne (1996) identified (among a range of key issues) this friction between inspectors and providers about the role of local councils. A further injustice, as care providers saw it, was that the 1984 Act provided councils with enforcement powers to ensure compliance by independent providers and prosecute where necessary, but this power did not extend to council services. A report would be sent to the director of social services, but that often seemed to be an end to a regulatory episode. However, some units, particularly those that were accountable to the chief executive, undertook follow-up and issued statutory notices to the director to apply pressure for non-compliance and to demonstrate the unit's independence. The units themselves were monitored by the Department of Health Social Services Inspectorate (SSI) in England, Social Services Inspectorate, Wales (SSIW) and the respective inspectorates in Scotland and Northern Ireland. Indeed, in England all 'arm's lengths units' were themselves inspected by SSI during the 1990s.

These central government inspectorates had separate inspection programmes of social care services provided by local councils not covered by regulatory legislation, for example, child protection services, sensory impairment or home care. One agreed outcome was to promote good practice and inspectors provided feedback with a local report. An action plan (with timescales) was then followed up with further sanctions (for non-compliance) available to the inspectorate if necessary. A national overview report was published to spread the findings and promote good practice.

In the regulated social care world the clamour for 'more independence' on the part of the arm's length local authority regulators continued (often fuelled by debates about fees and the growing role of local councils as commissioners of services). Following the scandal of abuse of residents in a regulated service in Buckinghamshire ('Longcare', Bucks CC 1994) and alleged failure of local regulation in that instance, an enquiry chaired by Tom Burgner recommended a fundamental shift away from local regulation in favour of a national framework of inspection (Burgner 1996). This coincided with a review of the role of local councils as social services authorities based on evidence from SSI/SSIW and 'Joint Review' (SSI/SSIW and Audit Commission) reports about social care services for children and adults.

The Care Standards Act 2000 (CSA) led to a fundamental shift in the inspection of all services regulated under the previous legislation in England and Wales. The responsibilities of local councils and health authorities (Joint Boards in Northern Ireland) for these services transferred under the Care Standards Act (2000) in England to the National Care Standards Commission (NCSC), a non-departmental public body, in 2001. In Wales the transfer was to an arm of the Wales Assembly Government – the Care Standards Inspectorate for Wales (CSIW), in 2002, and in Scotland to the Care Commission in 2002. Scotland and Northern Ireland have separate legislation in the Regulation of Care (Scotland) Act 2001 and the Health and Personal Social Service Quality, Improvement and Regulation (Northern Ireland) Order 2003, which set up the Regulation and Quality Improvement Authority (RQIA).

These changes in the regulation of health and social care across the UK were significant in many ways, but not least in that they brought policy development, policy implementation, monitoring and review to the regional/national government level and with them new forms of representation, participation and accountability. It also widened and made more explicit the regulatory functions of the new national bodies as well as the statutory duties and accountabilities placed on providers of services.

With the benefit of hindsight it may be that the relative insularity of social services departments, and the unimpeachability of the NHS, diverted attention away from the recognition of regulation as a significant policy option in welfare state strategies. However, it was during the 1980s that the Audit Commission became a key instrument of government policy (Henkel 1991; Power 1997), and the subsequent shift to regional government regulation of care services must be viewed in the light of the gathering momentum of the use of regulation to attain social and public policy objectives. It is currently a major issue for the NHS by virtue of the regulatory requirements of the Health and Social Care (Community Health and Standards) Act 2003 which now requires all NHS services to be regulated.

The mid-1990s saw initial joint inspections with the national inspectorates in England and Wales. Subsequently a programme of 'Joint Reviews' of social care services was established. Star ratings were developed (in England) and indicators for quality standards were used as an aid to organisational change. Low performance ratings and zero stars led to significant follow-up action by inspectorates. Local councils with outlying poor performance were subject to much greater challenge than ever before under the Local Government Act 1999 provisions for Joint Review and the new duty of Best Value.

The overall momentum of regulation may be associated with an ever more audited accountability for the operation of internal systems of service organisations. These processes have been criticised as potentially undermining the trust required of operators/providers and clearly reflect a new phase in the operation of a democratic, open society (Hansson 2006). Inspectors and their regulators are clearly mindful of this and seek to address it in inspection methodologies.

Inspection systems across the UK

The developing approach to regulation across the UK has been heavily influenced by the process of devolution in Wales and Scotland. In Northern Ireland the political process has led to a slower pace of change but a new regulatory body is now in place and assuming full duties. In England the Health and Social Care (Community Health and Standards) Act 2003 abolished the NCSC with effect from 31 March 2004 and its responsibilities for independent health care services transferred to the Commission for Healthcare Audit and Inspection, the 'The Healthcare Commission'. The regulation of early years services for children in England had always been located with Ofsted, unlike the arrangements in Wales and Scotland where regulation was integrated with other services. A new regulatory body in England, the Commission for Social Care Inspection (CSCI) took up its duties on 1 April 2004 and quickly undertook a review of its approach to regulation and the way in which an 'input approach' to inspection was less in tune with service user expectations about change and positive outcomes. It also absorbed the SSI and continued the development of inspection and assessment systems for non-regulated local council services.

Other restructuring in England has seen CSCI transferring its responsibilities for children's services to Ofsted (a non-ministerial government body established under the Education (Schools) Act 1992), in April 2007. The sheer scale of early years regulation, following the Care Standards Act 2000, had meant that Ofsted had already taken much of this role through joint inspections. Its responsibilities for adult services are planned to transfer and integrate with the Healthcare Commission and the Mental Health Act Commission to form a new 'Care Quality Commission' in 2009 subject to legislation currently in parliament.

In Scotland and Wales there has been a political desire to develop an integrated approach to public services. The position in Northern Ireland has changed more slowly but the Regulation and Quality Improvement Authority (RQIA) has now assumed its full range of responsibilities. In Wales the overall policy for health and social care is based upon the principle of integrated service planning and delivery, according to a 'whole system' approach. Within this context ministers have stressed the policy objective of partnership with local authorities and the voluntary sector, as well as the involvement of users. The aim has been to achieve a seamless service at the point of use. Accordingly politicians resisted the integration of inspectorates in 2003, viewing the distinctive contribution that they could make to locally responsive policies as being a priority. This policy should also be viewed within the broader strategy in Wales of maintaining direct government involvement in welfare, evidenced by the abolition of registration fees throughout the regulated sector and the recent introduction of free prescriptions. Changes in Wales have included the transfer of CSIW's responsibilities for independent health care services to the Healthcare Inspectorate Wales (1 April 2006) and the merger in April 2007 of CSIW and the SSIW to form the Care and Social Services Inspectorate, Wales.

In spite of policy divergence across the UK, the Westminster government's reform of regulation has continued to have an impact on policy and practice in Wales. The Better Regulation Executive's emphasis on the need for a proportionate approach to regulation is reflected in the Concordat reached between bodies inspecting, regulating and auditing health and social care in Wales (Welsh Assembly Government 2005). As in England, there has also been much more emphasis placed on the importance of the experience of users of regulated services and a focus on outcomes. The Beecham Review (2006) of public services in Wales recommended the location of regulation within a citizen focused public service in Wales (Welsh Assembly Government 2006). In Wales these reports have been instrumental in taking forward a reform agenda which places much more emphasis on the experience of users of regulated services and a focus on outcomes. A more proportionate inspection model also looks to providers engaging in more self-assessment of their service and inspection findings linked to an improvement agenda. The annual report of CSIW (2006) makes specific reference to engaging more with service users.

In England the shifting structural base has also not inhibited a progressive approach to reform undertaken by CSCI. It has fundamentally reviewed its methodologies and consulted widely on changes to inspection frequencies. It has also undertaken significant work to engage effectively with service users, and this includes a proportionate element of self-reporting. The CSCI annual report (2006a) develops this approach. Its chair, Denise Platt, states: 'It is not enough simply to ask people their views and tick the consultation box' (CSCI

2006b). The Children's Rights Director has published several important reports about the views of children and young people and what they want to see from inspection of the service they use, e.g. *Children's Views on Standards* (CSCI 2006b). On 1 April 2007 the Office of the Children's Rights Director transferred to Ofsted with all other services for children and young people.

In Scotland an approach to regulatory reform is developing with an increasing focus on an outcomes agenda engaging the experiences of service users. There is not as yet any proposal to change the current responsibilities of the Care Commission. In Northern Ireland the new RQIA will no doubt begin to reflect other parts of the UK in developing a reform direction suited to its own needs.

The process of inspection

The inspection process itself is a key element in this shift. The time taken for an inspection is influenced by the size of the establishment or agency – clearly a childminder will require less time than a large residential care home or home care agency. Prior knowledge from the registration phase and any previous inspections are also important since they can enable inspectors to target key issues. Typically inspection involves a combination of self-assessment, desk-based evidence gathered by inspectors, site visits and meetings between inspectors and providers, staff, service users and others (e.g. local council commissioners) and then a process of reporting.

There has been more contact with service users over time and their experiences have increasingly helped to inform judgements about services. Inspectors also judge performance in terms of standards laid down in Acts and Regulations and National Minimum Standards. Inspection reports typically identify any breaches of regulatory requirements and other areas for improvement. The action which follows from a report varies according to the nature of any deficiencies. Where the safety of vulnerable service users is at risk, compliance can be required within a 24-hour timescale and in some high risk situations inspectors can take immediate action to safeguard and protect vulnerable users by an application to the courts for closure. Generally, however, national inspectorates have been improvement oriented, requiring and recommending appropriate action over time.

The process of the inspection phase from analysis of self-assessment data from the provider through contact with key stakeholders, site visits, dialogue and report seeks to establish not only compliance to regulations and relevant minimum standards but also service improvements and positive outcomes for those using the service.

Much of the development work since 2000 undertaken by national inspectorates has focused on using the established data sets linked to identify issues in service improvement, but with clearer emphasis on the active role of the service provider. An inspection methodology linked to outcomes can be measured genuinely from an informed 'insider' standpoint, and is not simply an interpretation of the inspector.

There are rules of Common Law which govern the activities of inspectors and failure to abide by these can mean that the inspector and registration authority may be:

- liable to complaints and actions for damages in relation to damage caused

- failing to succeed on a prosecution for obstruction

- failing to be able to rely upon material obtained, at least in criminal proceedings (Ridout 2003, p.289).

The new focus of inspection

The modernising agenda of recent UK governments has had a significant impact on the regulation of social care. There has been significant structural change in all four countries of the UK, and all inspectorates have responded to Better Regulation Executive (BRE) reports by reviewing their inspection methodologies. But the impact of inspection can only be assessed within the broader regulatory relationships and performance outcomes that it seeks to influence.

By using a proportionate risk assessed approach a focus on issues that need to be inspected will be achieved. Through dialogue with inspectors and use of self-assessment information providers have accepted their responsibility under statute for not only their fitness, but also for service improvement. Inspection findings lead to judgements about improvement in outcomes which then become the responsibility of the provider to deliver.

The literature is full of descriptions of 'regulatory capture' where the procedures and consequent strategies of management that regulation (particularly inspection) promotes become, in reality, the ends of the regulatory relationship, rather than its means. To this notion Walshe (2002) has added the view of the 'deterrence' and 'compliance' regulatory relationships, where the service provider can be identified in terms of the extent to which they willingly comply with and deliver appropriate regulatory outcomes, as opposed to the situation where the inspector is the dreaded authority figure whose power will invariably dictate the next stage in the regulatory game. Indicators used to measure the extent of compliance with regulatory requirements have been subject to frequent criticism of imprecision and lacking in robustness, etc. (Freeman 2006).

We are currently in a phase where regulation is moving beyond reliance on 'inspection' to a new stage of maturity that is based on evidence of governance and dialogues, where the skill for the inspector will be to contribute to the locus of internal control within the service in such a way that the links between functional areas and stakeholder actions become more the focus of interest. This will be an agenda that is based on dialogue and open acknowledgement of what needs to change, in a culture of exploration of how change might take place. Inspectors have developed improved strategies to engage with service users and are better informed about their expressly desired outcomes. Taken together inspections are progressively moving from a quality control model to one of broader quality assurance.

Published annual inspectorate reports suggest that the focus of new methodologies is having an impact. More services are meeting national minimum standards and a more targeted approach theoretically means less regulatory activity and fewer inspection hours required. Inspectorates have reduced certain inspection frequencies, particularly where the service has 'scored' well at the preceding inspection. Governments can claim that the burden on service providers is being reduced and yet the public is still protected by a more efficient and effective inspection regime – albeit, as news headlines periodically emphasise, there are examples where even the best inspection methodology does not protect. The skill then is to focus on ways wherein the service provider is able to identify with the values represented by the regulator, and freely subscribes to these, for example, through 'Statements of Purpose' being set out as clear visioning and mission statements about the service. Information giving, supportive encouragement, target setting and rewards are all part of the regulatory repertoire. But to ensure requisite protection and service improvement the proportionate deployment of legal requirements that carry the threat of sanction will continue to be a response by the regulator where the services provided are deficient.

Future challenges

Martin (2005) suggests that public service inspectorates have been very successful in meeting the information needs of the present government but that:

> Because the policy agenda has developed so rapidly, inspection frameworks have been in an almost constant state of change over the last seven years. Performance measures and inspection criteria have been constantly tinkered with. (Martin 2005, p.501)

As the reform agenda unfolds in the different parts of the UK there will continue to be changes and challenges for regulators of social care. The broad principles outlined in recent government reports (such as those published by the Better Regulation Executive, the Office of Public Services Reform (OPSR) and the Hampton Review) suggest several key themes that will need to be addressed by the inspectorates:

1. The development of proportionate models of risk-based inspection which reduce detailed inspection but test the quality of service delivery.

2. The use of methodologies that combine self-assessment together with other forms of evidence, including that from other regulators and local commissioners of services, together with service user views, to inform judgements and convey the importance of the provider's own quality assurance systems.

3. Shaping regulatory methodologies for children and adult services so that the public and service users are assured about the continued fitness of both the service and provider through targeted inspection and enforcement action.

4. Developing regulatory models in line with principles of transparency, proportionality, consistency and cost effectiveness.

5. Equipping inspectors with a skill set which will ensure that regulation is effective, reflects engagement with public and

administrative law, as well as concepts, processes and procedures in regulatory practice. This will include processes of engaging more fully with service users and providers, enhancing the overall regulatory process and its responsiveness to choices and rights.

The experience of inspectors of the newly formed Care and Social Services Insopectorate Wales (CSSIW), who have undertaken a programme of approved training, is beginning to demonstrate the benefits of this approach.

The ongoing attempts to refine a systematic approach to the protection of vulnerable people in health and social care systems in the UK can draw upon databases of the inspectorates that provide an overview of the track record of services. Inspections are now developing according to a targeted and proportionate methodology which legally and practically requires the provider to assess their own capabilities and compliance. Ultimately we would argue that it is the dialogues that take place between providers, service users and the regulator that are the most important test of the effectiveness of inspection and ongoing improvement of the care service – not the arbitrariness of output measurements, over time or otherwise. The ability to apply enforcement sanctions and incentives is also an important means of securing compliance.

The end of our chapter is a timely point to recall that in 2000 a 'Regulation and Investigatory Powers Act 2000' was enacted which enables covert surveillance when this is deemed to be necessary to an investigation. The protection of vulnerable children and adults needs to be the overriding priority, but it is only attainable within the context of a tolerant and caring society that effectively 'signs up' to civilised outcomes. Political will and the self-identity of regulators must pay more attention to this dimension rather than selling out to the incident and crisis dimension of care.

References

Baldock P. (2001) *Regulating Early Years Services.* London: David Fulton.

Burgner, T. (1996) *The Regulation and Inspection of Social Services.* London: Department of Health and the Welsh Office.

Butler, I. and Drakeford, M. (2003) *Social Policy, Social Welfare and Scandal: How British Public Policy is Made.* London: Palgrave.

Care Standards Inspectorate for Wales (CSIW, 2006) *Annual Report.* Cardiff: Welsh Assembly Government.

Clarke Hall, W. (1926) *Children's Courts.* London: Allen and Unwin.

Commission for Social Care Inspection (CSCI, 2006a) *Annual Report and Accounts.* London: The Stationery Office.

Commission for Social Care Inspection (CSCI, 2006b) *Children's Views on Standards.* London: The Stationery Office.

Davies, C. (2000) 'Frameworks for Regulation and Accountability: Threat or Opportunity?' In A. Brechin, H. Brown and M. A. Eby (eds) *Critical Practice in Health and Social Care.* London: Sage.

Davison, A. (1995) *Residential Care: The Provision of Quality Care in Residential Group Care Settings.* Aldershot: Arena.

Day, P. and Klein, R. (1990) *Inspecting the Inspectorates.* York: Joseph Rowntree.

Day, P., Klein, R. and Redmayne, S. (1996) *Why Regulate?* Bristol: The Policy Press.

Freeman, T. (2006) 'Performance Measurement and Improvement.' In K. Walshe and J. Smith (eds) *Healthcare Management.* Maidenhead: Open University Press.

Hansson, F. (2006) 'Organisational use of evaluations.' *Evaluation 12,* 1, 159–178.

Henkel, M. (1991) *Government, Evaluation and Change.* London: Jessica Kingsley Publishers.

Jackson, J. *et al.* (eds) (1997) *Clarke Hall and Morrison on Children,* 9th edn. London: Butterworth.

MacLeod, M. (1999) 'The Abuse of Children in Institutional Settings.' In N. Stanley, J. Manthorpe and B. Penhale (eds) *Institutional Abuse: Perspectives Across the Life Course.* London: Routledge.

Martin, S.J. (2005) 'Evaluation, inspection and the improvement agenda: Contrasting fortunes in an era of evidence-based policy-making.' *Evaluation 11,* 4, 496–504.

Petrie, P. (2003) 'Social Pedagogy: An Historical Account of Care and Education as Social Control.' In J. Brannen and P. Moss (eds) *Rethinking Children's Care.* Maidenhead: Open University Press.

Power, M. (1997) *The Audit Society: Rituals of Verification.* Oxford: Oxford University Press.

Pring, J. (2003) *Silent Victims: The Continuing Failure to Protect Society's Most Vulnerable and The Longcare Scandal.* London: Gibson Square Books.

Ridout, P. (1998) *Registered Homes.* Bristol: Jordans.

Ridout, P. (2003) *Care Standards: A Practical Guide.* Bristol: Jordans.

Smith, J. (1972) *A Brief Guide to Social Legislation.* London: Methuen.

Taylor, A. (1998) 'Hostages to Fortune: The Abuse of Children in Care.' In G. Hunt (ed.) *Whistleblowing in the Social Services: Public Accountability and Professional Practice.* London: Arnold.

Wagner (Lady) (1988) *Report of the Independent Review of Residential Care.* London: HMSO.

Walshe, K. (2002) 'The rise of regulation in the NHS', *British Medical Journal 324,* 967–970.

Wardough, J. and Wilding, P. (1993) 'Towards an explanation of the corruption of care.' *Critical Social Policy 13,* 37, 4–31.

Waterhouse, Sir R. (2000) *Lost in Care: Report of the Tribunal of Inquiry into the Abuse of Children in Care in the Former County Council Areas of Gwynedd and Clwyd since 1974.* London: Stationery Office.

Welsh Assembly Government (2006) *Beyond Boundaries: Citizen-centered Local Services for Wales.* Cardiff: Welsh Assembly Government.

CHAPTER 4

Inspection of Education and Skills
From Improvement to Accountability

Jane Martin

The evolution of inspection arrangements for education and skills

The public inspection of schools probably has the longest history of all the formal inspectorates. It is a history that has over the years reflected the developing system of state education, the shifts in power between central and local government, the development of the teaching profession and more recent trends towards the participation of parents and learners. What has characterised the organisation of inspectorates and the processes of inspection has, however, been a consistent focus on quality assurance of educational institutions – schools, colleges and latterly nurseries – and, in the case of skills, institutional provision in the workplace.

The first inspectors of schools were appointed under the Factory Act of 1833 with the power to establish schools for children working in the factories. This role developed into an inspection function to gather information and report back to the government on the implementation of the educational clauses of legislation. Inspection procedures subsequently developed for church schools. During the nineteenth century Her Majesty's Inspectorate (HMI), of whom one distinguished member was Matthew Arnold, developed a reputation for encouraging the development of teachers and high standards of scholarship. By the end of the century HMI had a clear remit from government 'not to inflict penalties for defective points, but rather through your educational suggestions and influence to remove defects in the school management and instruction' (Brighouse and Moon 1995, p.6).

At a local level, the new schools boards created by the Forster Act 1870 had responsibility for the efficiency of their schools and began to employ inspectors of their own. In the early twentieth century, the local education authorities inherited this system of local inspection, described in a National Union of Teachers (NUT) circular to HMI in 1908 as 'on the whole a hindrance rather than an aid to educational progress' (Brighouse and Moon 1995, p.8). By the 1970s, following the establishment of the system of universal education in 1945 and the increased responsibilities of local education authorities for the management and administration of schools, local inspection and advice grew with the further provision of curriculum specialist advisers. The Balfour Act 1902 had established the principle that all secondary schools should be inspected by HMI but these had virtually ceased by the 1950s with the government giving way to local provision which tended towards a collegiate approach to curriculum support for teachers. Indeed it was the so-called 'secret garden' of the curriculum, regarded as the increasingly professionalised domain of the teacher, coupled with concerns about local political influence in education, which prompted the call for independent and transparent evaluation of schools in the Jim Callaghan's Ruskin Speech of 1976.

We can attribute current structures and systems of inspection across the UK to the education reforms of the 1980s. The Education Acts of 1980, 1986 and 1988 introduced a new system of delegated management of schools whereby every school would be required to have a governing body (which included a majority of parents) responsible for the local management of the school and the delivery of a new national curriculum and testing system. The new system was driven by the key principle of opening up the education system to greater public accountability within the context of informed parental choice of school. Education reform which stripped the local education authority of its responsibility for school management and administration, and relied on better public information on school effectiveness and pupil achievement required an independent evidence-based inspection system. In May 1993 the Office for Standards in Education (Ofsted) was created as a non-governmental body, independent of the Secretary of State, with the expressed purpose to 'improve standards of achievement and quality of education through regular independent inspection, public reporting and informed advice' (Brighouse and Moon, p.35). Its formation met the brief to generate greater openness and transparency and also responded to national concerns about poor education performance and the lack of regular and robust quality assurance. While the HMI of the 1950s and 1960s had a role to promote and disseminate good practice and inform government about the quality of education, the role of Ofsted was to evaluate and challenge schools to improve and make public their judgements. What followed was a rigorous regime of regular evidence-based inspections of all maintained schools against a national standards framework with published reports and mandatory action planning. Schools causing the most concern were labelled as having 'serious weaknesses' and put into 'special measures' for improvement or risk closure.

Inspection systems across the UK

Inspection arrangements in the different countries of the UK reflect their different contexts. In England and Wales, inspection is a key vehicle for public information and accountability within a system where parents exercise choice in selecting a school for their child, the so-called 'market' in education. This has been described as 'accountability through consumer information' (OECD/ CERI 1995, p.55). In Northern Ireland inspection the focus is more on quality assurance within a selective system. In Scotland, the role of the inspectorate is to support schools within a comprehensive system.

In Northern Ireland educational performance in schools is monitored and inspected by the Education and Training Inspectorate (ETI) whose main function is to keep ministers and officials in the Department of Education for Northern Ireland informed on all aspects of education. The Education Reform Order 1989 summarises the purposes of ETI as: to promote high standards; inspect, monitor and report on educational outcomes of schools and colleges; report on the quality of support services offered by the education and library boards; and to report inspection findings to the Department of Education.

In Scotland, the role of Her Majesty's Scottish Inspectorate of Education (HMIE) has continued in a similar vein to HMI with continued emphasis on support for curriculum development and school improvement. In April 2001 it became an independent executive agency working within the Standards in Scotland's Schools Act 2000. Under the devolved administration of the Scottish Parliament, HMIE now has statutory powers to inspect the education function of local authorities as well as preschool education, primary and secondary schools, teacher education, community learning and development, and further education colleges. Its remit is to evaluate how well the new legislation is being implemented and to provide professional advice to raise standards (www.hmie.gov.uk/hmie.asp).

There has been a distinct Welsh inspectorate since 1907. It is charged with inspecting elementary and secondary schools. Esteem was created in 1998 as the office of Her Majesty's Chief Inspector of Education and Training in Wales under Section 104 of the Government of Wales Act. It is funded by the National Assembly for Wales but independent of it and is responsible for conducting statutory inspections and reporting on education and training providers. This is a comprehensive brief which covers nursery schools, all schools, colleges, local education authorities (LEAs), teacher education and workplace training. Drawing on its independent evidence base it provides advice to the Minister of Education, Lifelong Learning and Skills.

In England, Ofsted works in partnership with the Adult Learning Inspectorate (ALI) the independent skills inspectorate created under the Learning and Skills Act 2000 and the Independent Schools Inspectorate (ISI) created by the Education Act 2000 under an Ofsted approved framework. The Adult Learning Inspectorate (ALI) inspects all work-based learning and adult learning provided by the Department for Children, Schools and Families (DCSF) and other government departments such as for the armed services, prisons and young offenders institutions for people over the age of 16 and for those over the age of 19 studying in further education colleges.

In April 2007 the remit of Ofsted was expanded to cover the full range of childcare and education provision for children and young people, as well as learning and skills provision for learners of all ages. The organisation was reconfigured to include the inspection of children's social care, formerly the responsibility of the Commission for Social Care Inspection (CSCI), the inspection of the Children and Family Court Advisory and Support Service, formerly undertaken by Her Majesty's Inspectorate of Court Administration, the inspection services of the ALI as well as the inspection of schools and initial teacher training. This move was part of the creation of four 'super-inspectorates' to streamline the inspection of public services provided by 11 inspectorates in England.

School inspections in the UK have typically required a visit of anything from one day to a week, depending on the size of the school and the inspectorate. They are carried out at regular intervals, Ofsted having the shortest cycle with inspections every three years, and Her Majesty's Inspectorate of Education (HMIe) having the longest cycle with its inspection of Scottish primary schools on a seven-year basis. Although each inspectorate has its own inspection framework, they follow similar guidelines, with a focus on four main areas during inspections: effectiveness and achievement; support for pupils; quality of the learning environment; and leadership and management of the school. Inspections teams vary from one to five inspectors.

Inspectors gather a variety of information for an inspection. Preliminary research can include the study of schools' self-evaluation forms, questionnaires completed by parents, carers and pupils (where appropriate), and the review of prior inspection reports. Inspectors meet head teachers and senior staff, and can then meet with staff and visit classes to evaluate learning, teaching and aspects of achievement. Meetings with groups of pupils may also be organised during visits. A lay member may be included in the inspection team, but is usually not involved in evaluating professional aspects of the school's operations. Inspectors then produce a report, which is made public and sent to relevant partners, including the school authority, the head teacher and the local authority.

Inspectors follow through their report with recommendations. Ofsted has four grades by which it judges the quality of an institution: outstanding, good, satisfactory and inadequate. Schools not performing well enough can thus be placed under 'special measures' or are given a 'notice to improve'. Schools must produce an action plan to improve, against which progress is monitored. Under special measures this follow-up process can proceed until the inspectorate deems that the school is providing an acceptable standard of education (Ofsted 1999).

A range of resources exists to support improvement. All of the inspectorates provide an online version of their inspection reports, and publish annual reports (bi-annual in the case of ETI). They provide information about the inspection process, with separate guidance for school governors or head teachers, parents and teachers. They provide guidelines for self-evaluation by schools, benchmarking documents, and reports giving specific advice on particular subjects such as special needs teaching or drugs guidance. The ALI also maintains a library of good practice examples from across the adult learning sector, and provides a qualification that recognises a Quality Champion's contribution to improvement. New arrangements for school inspections were implemented by Ofsted from September 2005 which brought in more frequent inspections undertaken by few inspectors who spend no more than two days in the school and use the school's self-evaluation and performance data at the starting point for a dialogue with senior management. This 'light touch' inspection follows a shorter notice period to avoid unnecessary pre-inspection preparation and is intended to help inspectors see schools as they really are. In the academic year 2005–06 Ofsted conducted over 6000 inspections of maintained schools.

The impact of inspection

Any analysis of the impact of inspection should be predicated on a clear understanding of the primary purposes and focus of the process. Reference to the corporate documents of the education and skills inspectorates across the UK variously underlines the purposes as follows:

> To serve the interests of children and young people, their parents and the community by providing impartial and authoritative inspection, evaluation and reporting of the quality and standards of education and childcare. (Ofsted 2004, p.5)

> To inspect and report on the quality of training, raise standards by sharing inspection knowledge and offer independent quality assessment. (www.ali.gov.uk)

> To inspect quality and standards in education and training. (Estyn 2006–09, p.1)

> Independent, rigorous evaluation of the education system contributing to improvement and leading to independent advice on educational policy. (HMIE 2003, p.6)

It is also important to clarify the focus of the inspection process. Inspections make judgements about the quality and standards of educational institutions and providers. In this respect the impact of inspection is primarily on the performance of the institution. This could be defined as the *effectiveness* of the institution – the extent to which the institution is effective in ensuring high standards of pupil performance and achievement – as well as the capacity of the institution to *improve* – the institutional standards of teaching, management, leadership, governance and teaching.

As Wilcox and Gray (1996) point out, the creation of a comprehensive and national system of school inspection in the early 1990s was something of an experiment, with a very limited evidence base. Much of the research literature since then which has analysed the inspection process has been focused on two areas of concern: first, the methodology and process of inspection and its impact on school improvement; second, the effect of inspection in terms of improved outcomes for teachers and pupils.

The methodology and process of inspection

The prime methodology of an inspection is to gather evidence, focused on a visit to the institution, on which to make judgements about standards and performance. The dominant model is for the institution to provide a written submission to an inspection team who then agree a series of interviews and observations during an intensive short visit which includes opportunities for parents and pupils to make their views known. Based on the evidence collected, inspectors produce an evaluative report with recommendations for improvement which the school is required to implement through an action planning process.

Particularly in its early days Ofsted inspections were seen as having negative effects on staff morale and this became a major cause for concern. Research carried out by the National Foundation for Educational Research (NFER) for the NUT drew attention to the stress and anxiety suffered by teachers during the inspection process of schools placed in 'special measures' (Scanlon 1999). In a study of 24 inspections, Gray and Wilcox (1995) found evidence of persistent teacher anxiety even in schools in receipt of a good inspection report. Lonsdale and Parsons (Earley 1998) also document the extent of the disruption caused by early Ofsted inspections which, it was claimed lasted four or five months in one school. The experience of inspection depends on a number of factors, however, ranging from: the quality of the inspection team; the relationships between inspectors and the governing body, the head teacher and staff; the capacity of the school to prepare for the inspection; and the extent to which the school is judged to need to improve. While the methodology of the school visit is consistent across the UK as a vehicle for inspection, it should not, however, be assumed that the particular experience of the early Ofsted approach is typical.

Other concerns with the process of inspection have included questions about the appropriateness of the methodology for gathering relevant data and making evaluative judgements. Fitzgibbon (1998, p.22) has asserted that 'Ofsted's judgements are seriously inaccurate and highly damaging to schools' because of flaws in the methodology and unreliability of the data evidence collected. The extent to which a short inspection visit divorced from in-depth knowledge of the context and culture of the school can be the basis of a sound evaluation has also been questioned. Associated concerns with sampling techniques used to select classroom observations and pupils' work have led to challenges that such a qualitative and inevitably subjective evaluation may not be 'true' (Gray and Wilcox 1995). From the perspectives of all concerned, as Ferguson *et al.* (2000, p.16) suggest, 'the nature of the Ofsted judgement process is determined by the highly concentrated and very intense nature of an inspection'.

Inspection as a driver for improvement

One of the key functions of inspection in the education and skills sector is to raise standards. Original guidance for inspectors in 1840 included the need to say 'what improvements in the apparatus and internal management of schools, in school management and discipline, and in the methods of teaching have been sanctioned by the most extensive experience'.[1] It is, however, difficult to establish any causal link between inspection and improvement. While recognising the benefits of the inspection process in providing objective feedback and prompting action planning for improvement, several studies have raised the question of the disjunction between a challenging inspection process and a supportive improvement process (Earley 1998). Evaluating the performance of educational institutions in terms of their strengths and weaknesses is a valuable exercise but does not of itself lead to improvement. As highlighted in an international study of seven OECD countries:

> Without follow-up advice and monitoring to help a school to improve, a sound programme of teacher development which takes the morale of the teaches into account, a real understanding of how institutions work and

---

1   For more on this see Estyn (2006). Available at www.hmie.gov.uk, accessed 16 June 2007

how to manage change, and more willingness on the part of the authorities to put resources into schools with problems, post-evaluation improvement in many schools is likely to be short-term and limited. (OECD 1995, pp.24–25)

Studies seeking to understand if and how schools had improved as a result of inspection have proved inconclusive. Shaw *et al.* (2003) interrogated examination performance data and concluded that Ofsted inspection had no positive effect on examination achievement and may have had a detrimental effect. Reflecting on the impact of inspection recommendations as a catalyst for change and improvement, Wilcox and Gray (1996) found that while recommendations could add authority and legitimacy to existing plans for improvement, the extent to which schools were able to respond effectively was uncertain and some recommendations were not treated as urgent or valid. Perhaps most crucially, they found that action planning was seen as a mundane process with little evidence of head teachers effectively turning inspection recommendations into broader strategies for improvement with the commitment of staff. In 2004 a report from Ofsted and the Institute of Education in London found that inspection was neither a catalyst for instant improvement in GCSE results nor a significant inhibitor, concluding that inspection has provided the evaluation, leverage and accountability that have helped to embed national strategies in educational practice, but that many schools do not always follow up or make the best use of inspection findings (Matthews and Sammons 2004).

This debate raises questions about the extent to which it should be the role of the inspectorate to help schools self-evaluate. As Macbeath (1999) has argued, the goal of raising standards will best be achieved 'by helping schools to know themselves, do it for themselves and to give their own account of their achievements' (p.2). As an evaluative process, weaknesses in the 'snapshot' approach have more recently been addressed by introducing school self-evaluation as part of inspection. This development has generally been welcomed and is acknowledged as being of value in focusing on and driving improvement (Matthews and Sammons 2004; Pricewaterhousecoopers 2006).

The most recent evaluation of the work of Ofsted, reported in May 2007, reflected on the impact of inspection across their brief from early years to initial teacher training (Ofsted 2007a). The report concludes that the relationship between inspection and improvement is not simple and that the former cannot categorically be said to lead to the latter. Indeed, it is acknowledged that it is the leaders, managers, staff, children and young people who use the services who bring about improvement. In this regard the importance of the dialogue around self-evaluation is highlighted. The key findings from this extensive study propose the following:

- Providers themselves make the improvements; inspection and regulation act as a catalyst.

- Inspection and regulation make a difference to individual providers and to provision nationally, although this difference is uneven.

- Inspection and regulation generate considerable public interest and make providers accountable to users and the wider community.

- Considerable progress had been made in the last three years in reducing the cost of inspection, in targeting resources more effectively and in engaging with providers.

- Providers found to be inadequate usually improve rapidly and stronger providers also make good progress; however, too many stand still or decline.

- Engaging institutions directly in the process of inspection and regulation has increased their understanding of their performance and set the context for further improvement.

- Providers value dialogue with inspectors, gain confidence when their judgements and those of inspectors coincide and are better able to set priorities for improvement.

- Inspection of aspects of provision has made a difference across the system as a whole, contributing to national policy and to decisions about spending on education priorities (Ofsted 2007a, pp.3–4).

Drilling down beneath these headlines reveals positive feedback on the inspection process from those being inspected:

Most respondents agree that by creating a framework of accountability, by improving the practice of self-evaluation, by encouraging dialogue throughout the inspection, by testing or confirming an institution's view of itself and by clarifying how it can improve, Ofsted has made a difference. (Ofsted 2007a, p.7)

Reflecting on the revised inspection process for schools since September 2005 (Section 5 inspections), the NFER concluded that nearly two-thirds of survey respondents and just over half the case study interviewees considered that the inspection had contributed to school improvement by confirming, prioritising and clarifying areas for improvement rather than by highlighting new areas (McCrone *et al.* 2007). Here again, however, the importance of the self-evaluation process was highlighted.

The future
Ensuring 'fitness for purpose' in times of expansion and change

A number of pressures have resulted in government focusing on 'better regulation' through rationalisation of the national inspectorates. Service providers have been calling for the burden of inspection to be lifted and a greater focus on self-evaluation and risk-based inspection. Government has become increasingly concerned with value for money and the need to cut the costs of inspection. Inspectors have realised that inspection of public services needs a much more joined up approach and collaborative working.

Within this context, inspection has become one significant intervention within a wider continuous improvement landscape where education and skills training providers take responsibility for their own improvement and development, and inspection is delivered within partnership arrangements to hold providers accountable locally within national frameworks. This has placed inspectors increasingly in the role of enabling, supporting and reporting publicly on self-evaluation to inform public choice and policy direction.

As indicated above, the remit for Ofsted was expanded from April 2007 and rebranded as the inspection of children's social care. This is a continually shifting landscape with the introduction of a holistic children's services working with 'extended' schools providing 'wrap-around' care throughout the day including preschool facilities through Children's Centres. The expansion of preschool facilities is another area for which the expanded regulator has responsibility. A review of the National Minimum Standards for social care services is under way and one of the key issues for the new organisation will be how to ensure a smooth transition from the former inspectorates, in particular the CSCI.

Among its responsibilities Ofsted will carry out joint area reviews (JARs) and annual performance assessments of local children's services provision as well as inspection of the Children and Family Court Advisory and Support Service (CAFCASS). Each very different type of activity is looking at very different types of institutions and services. This will inevitably raise issues concerning the expertise of inspectors and the efficient organisation of a much greater workload. This also indicates a significant refocusing of the objectives of inspection as a vehicle for public accountability, building on its strengths for independent and objective evidence to evaluate and quality assure service provision. Impartial inspection reported 'without fear or favour' (Ofsted 2007b).

The Centre for Public Scrutiny (CfPS) has recommended four principles for good scrutiny which provide a useful framework for considering the future agenda for inspection of education and skills. The CfPS (2006) suggests that scrutiny should:

- provide 'critical friend' challenge to executive policymakers and decision-makers

- enable the voice and concerns of the public

- be carried out by 'independent minded governors' who lead and own the scrutiny role

- drive improvement in public services.

CRITICAL FRIEND CHALLENGE

One of the acknowledged benefits of current systems of inspection is the opportunity it creates for critical friend challenge to providers to reflect on past and current practice and make changes which will lead to future improvement. Debates about the appropriateness of whether inspection is generated from within the organisation or carried out by local or national inspectorates agree on the importance of constructive relationships between inspectors and those being inspectors to achieve improvement as well as the willingness of providers to open themselves up to robust public challenge including learners and their families. Consistent with the literature on learning organisations which promotes the importance of institutional reflection for improvement, the significance of external impulses creating 'pressure to improve' is recognised by Ehren and Visscher (2006) as one important element explaining the impact of inspection. The notion of critical friend is not new. Costa and Kallic defined it as: 'a trusted person, who asks provocative questions, provides data to be examined through another lens and offers critique of a person's work as a friend' (Macbeath and Mortimore 2001, p.139).

In the Improvement School Effectiveness Project, Macbeath and Mortimore adopted a critical friend approach to intervention and support in 24 schools, accepting that the role needed to be positively facilitative and supportive and not directive or evaluative (Macbeath and Mortimore 2001, p.139).

ENABLING THE VOICE AND CONCERNS OF THE PUBLIC

A clear trend in the development of inspection of education and skills has been the increasing involvement of all 'stakeholders', in particular parents and learners, in a more democratic approach to inspection. In comparison with other inspection models, practice in this area is probably more advanced, providing examples and lessons which others might follow. Including one trained 'lay' inspectors in the inspection team is an established part of the Ofsted model, replicated elsewhere across the UK, reinforcing the contribution of an informed member of the public. Meeting with parents in schools and canvassing their views through a questionnaire as part of the inspection process is now standard practice. The latter model, pioneered in the Quality Assurance Unit of Strathclyde Regional Council in the early 1990s, demonstrated the extent to which parents will contribute constructive criticism of value to the improvement process (Martin, Ranson and Tall 1997). More recent research suggests that while the parents who attend meetings with the inspector find it worthwhile, the numbers who attend are low (Matthews and Sammons 2004). In Wales, the inspectorate places a particular emphasis on increasing the involvement of learners in inspections through a commitment to 'listening to learners' and securing feedback on the experiences of users of the services (Estyn 2006).

AN INDEPENDENT AND OBJECTIVE VIEW

An acknowledged strength of inspection, and key to public accountability, has been the opportunity for an independent and objective view of education provision to be reported based on evidence against national standards. Prior to the establishment of a national curriculum, a key criticism was the lack of objective evaluation of the curriculum against transparent indicators. While the need for local and institutional variation in response to curriculum needs is now acknowledged, parents choosing providers welcome the public information made available through inspection reports to help them make judgements against objective criteria as part of their selection process. Inspectorates acknowledge the need to make their reporting even more accessible and their processes as open as possible, consistent with their role to share independent evaluations of providers with policymakers, practitioners and the public. A recent survey of parents revealed: 'Inspection evidence can be seen to enhance consumer confidence and many parents view school inspection as important to maintain and improve the quality of education.' For learners, 'Inspection can be seen to have a major role in representing and safeguarding their interests particularly in weak institutions with a history of problems' (Matthews and Sammons 2004, p.157).[2]

The role of national inspectorates in evaluating national systems based on independent data is an acknowledged source of advice and guidance for government. The annual report of the chief inspector is a key state of the nation report supplemented by ad hoc thematic, subject or sector specific reports. Such work provides the major source of evidence on standards and quality of the implementation of legislation and national strategies, such as the numeracy and literacy strategies.

DRIVING IMPROVEMENT IN PUBLIC SERVICES

Inspection is only one significant intervention in a process of continuous improvement. Moves towards risk-based inspection reinforce this. Where there is sufficient evidence of high standards and quality of provision then there is less need for expensive and stressful inspection intervention. Where there is cause for concern and insufficient evidence of institutional capacity to self-evaluate and improve, the need for intervention is greater. The future role for national inspectorates will be to support and develop self-evaluation rather than to evaluate. This suggests that the responsibility for improvement is shifting back to the institution. It is interesting to note the language of the Ofsted Strategic Plan 2005–8 which states the aim to 'establish effective inspection and regulation frameworks that meet the needs of all our stakeholders' with no specific mention of resulting improvement. While inspection must be a catalyst and facilitator of improvement it will no longer be expected to be the improvement mechanism. Inspection will continue to make an impact on performance as part of a system of public scrutiny which effects public

---

2   For example, see Clarke and Munn (1997, pp.115–116) and Matthews and Sammons (2004, p.107).

challenge and requires institutions to account for their own responsibilities to deliver quality standards and improve. This means regarding inspection as one important bit of the machinery. Often working together as, for example, Ofsted and the Audit Commission on comprehensive performance assessment of local authorities or with the ALI regarding the 14 to 19 curriculum, or the HMIE in Scotland and the Scottish Care Commission on preschool provision.

While recognising that inspection arrangements across the UK reflect the national systems of education in which they operate, their common purpose is to be an effective tool for public accountability. Through inspection, providers of education and skills training are answerable to the public for the services they provide and the public can be reassured of the quality of provision and, where applicable, make informed choices of access to provision.

References

Adult Learning Inspectorate (ALI, 2005) *Annual Report of the Chief Inspector 2004–5.* London: Adult Learning Inspectorate (www.ali.gov.uk).

Brighouse, T. and Moon, B. (1995) *School Inspection.* London: Pitman.

Centre for Public Scrutiny (CfPS, 2006) *The Good Scrutiny Guide,* 2nd edition. London: CfPS.

Clarke, M. and Munn, P. (1997) *Education in Scotland.* London: Routledge.

Earley, P. (1998) *School Improvement After Inspection?* London: Paul Chapman.

Ehren, M. C. M. and Visscher, A. J. (2006) 'Towards a theory of the impact of school inspections.' *British Journal of Education Studies 54,* 1, 51–72.

Estyn (2006) *Corporate Plan 2006–9.* Cardiff: Estyn.

Ferguson, N., Earley, P., Fidler, B. And Ouston, J. (2000) *Improving Schools and Inspection: The Self-Inspecting School.* London: Paul Chapman.

Fitzgibbon, C. (1998) 'Can Ofsted stay afloat?' *Managing Schools Today 7,* 6, 22–25.

Gray, C. and Gardner, J. (1999) 'The impact of school inspections.' *Oxford Review of Education 25,* 4.

Gray, J. and Wilcox, B. (1995) *Good School Bad School: Evaluating Performance and Encouraging Improvement.* Maidenhead: Open University Press.

Macbeath, J. (1999) *Schools Must Speak for Themselves: The Case for School Self-Evaluation.* London: Routledge.

Macbeath, J. and Mortimore, P. (2001) *Improving School Effectiveness.* Maidenhead: Open University Press.

Martin, J., Ranson, S. and Tall, G. (1997) 'Parents as partners in assuring the quality of schools.' *Scottish Educational Review 29,* 1, 39–55.

Matthews, P. and Sammons, P. (2004) *Improvement Through Inspection: An Evaluation of the Impact of Ofsted's Work, HMI 2244.* London: Ofsted.

McCrone, T., Rudd, P., Blenkinsop, S., Wade, P., Rutt, S. and Yeshanew, T. (2007) *Evaluation of the Impact of Section 5 Inspections.* Slough: NFER.

OECD/CERI (1995) *Schools Under Scrutiny.* Paris: OECD.

Ofsted (1999) *Lessons Learned from Special Measures.* London: Ofsted.

Ofsted (2004) *Strategic Plan 2005–8.* London: Ofsted.

Ofsted (2007a) *Review of the Impact of Inspection.* London: Ofsted.

Ofsted (2007b) *Raising Standards, Improving Lives: The Office for Standards in Education, Children's Services and Skills Strategic Plan 2007–10.* London: Ofsted.

Pricewaterhousecoopers (2006) *Estyn – Evaluation of Inspection Arrangements.* London: PWC.

Scanlon, M. (1999) *The Impact of Ofsted Inspections.* London: NFER.

Shaw, I., Newton, D.P., Aitkin, M. and Darnell, R. (2003) 'Do Ofsted inspections of secondary schools make a difference to GCSE results?' *British Educational Research Journal 29,* 1, 63–75.

Wilcox, B. and Gray, J. (1996) *Inspecting Schools: Holding Schools to Account and Helping Schools to Improve.* Maidenhead: Open University Press.

CHAPTER 5

Regulation and Inspection of Health Services

Kieran Walshe

Introduction

This chapter describes how the inspection and regulation of UK health services has developed over the last two decades, explores what is known about the effectiveness of those arrangements and their impact on health services performance, and discusses how inspection and regulation have changed and will change in the future.

The systems for inspection and regulation are not straightforward to present, for two reasons. First, there has been a longstanding divide between the oversight of the health services funded and provided by the British National Health Service (NHS) and those services provided by a wide range of other health care organisations and entities, and financed through private health insurance, direct payment by patients and other mechanisms. Effectively, two quite separate and different regulatory regimes have been in place for the private and public health care systems, though latterly they have been set on a path towards convergence in England. This leads to the second complication, which is that while the arrangements for inspection and regulation were essentially the same or very similar across the four UK countries up to the late 1990s, since the establishment of the devolved administrations for Scotland, Wales and Northern Ireland there has been a gradual divergence in health policy, health system structures and governance (Greer 2005), and in the arrangements for regulation and inspection. Now, different regulatory entities, legal frameworks and regimes operate in the four countries, and while many similarities remain there are important areas of difference.

Two further caveats to the content of this chapter are also worth noting. The chapter is focused on the regulation of health services, but the dividing line between health and social care regulation (covered in Chapter 3) is a shifting and sometimes contested boundary. For example, responsibility for the oversight of nursing and residential home care has in the past been divided between health authorities and local authorities, before being brought together in England first under the National Care Standards Commission (NCSC) and latterly under the aegis of the current social care regulator in England, the Commission for Social Care Inspection (CSCI). Furthermore, this chapter focuses on the regulation and inspection of organisations. It does not cover the equally important and interesting area of health professions regulation (Allsop and Saks 2003), by the nine statutory regulatory bodies (the General Medical Council, Nursing and Midwifery Council, Health Professions Council, and others) overseen by the Council for Healthcare Regulatory Excellence. But again, the boundary between organisational and professional regulation is not straightforward, since regulators like the Royal Pharmaceutical Society for Great Britain (RPSGB) and the General Optical Council have statutory powers to regulate both individual professionals and corporate bodies (for example, companies like Boots, Superdrug and Lloyds Chemists are all overseen by the RPSGB).

The history of regulation and inspection of the NHS

As a publicly funded, owned and managed health service, the NHS made relatively little use of statutory regulation for many years. Instead, it relied largely upon traditional bureaucratic central direction, with the Department of Health issuing instructions, guidance and rules to health authorities and NHS trusts through a blizzard of policy papers, health circulars, executive letters and other means every year. Conventional wisdom held that there was no need for a separate formal regulatory function in such a vertically integrated, directly managed structure, and indeed that regulation might conflict with or constrain the Department of Health's ability to run the NHS (Scrivens 1995).

Before 1980, the only real example of a regulator for the NHS was the Health Advisory Service. It was set up in 1969, as a result of a public inquiry into major problems with the quality of care at Ely Hospital, a long-stay institution in Cardiff. The inquiry report uncovered ill treatment, abuse and neglect of patients, resulting from poor staff training, little leadership, low clinical standards and resource constraints. Among its 44 recommendations, it proposed the creation of an inspectorate which would monitor the quality of care in long-stay institutions and take action to rectify their shortcomings (Department of Health and Social Security 1969). The then Secretary of State, Richard Crossman, pressed for its establishment against the wishes of his civil servants who did not want a formal inspectorate. (Crossman 1977).

Originally titled the Hospital Advisory Service, HAS formally reported direct to ministers, but saw itself as existing primarily to advise and support those in the health service, to spread good practice, and to promote improvement. It seemed to command considerable attention for its work for the first six or seven years of its life, but then its influence began to wane as health authorities grew accustomed to periodic visits, and learned to understand and perhaps to manage its interventions. As its political visibility and importance diminished, HAS became more and more reliant on the credibility of its regulatory process as its source of authority. However, that process was much criticised for features which resulted from its highly compliance-oriented, professionalised nature. It was argued that HAS reports were extremely variable in quality, that different teams would produce quite different findings and recommendations, and that there was no consistency in the visit process. In part this resulted from the absence of explicit standards, which also meant that findings were difficult to justify and often appeared subjective. It was also argued that the professional domination of the HAS process produced a rather closed and introspective form of review, in which other stakeholders – particularly patients or users – played little part (Day, Klein and Tipping 1988; Henkel et al. 1989).

There were other regulatory players in the British NHS at this time – the Audit Commission, originally created to oversee the performance of local government, gained new responsibilities for the oversight of value for money in health authorities from the early 1990s. The National Audit Office had (and still has) a statutory role as parliament's independent accounting and auditing body in relation to the Department of Health and the NHS. The Health Service Ombudsman undertook independent investigations into complaints about maladministration by NHS organisations which it reported to parliament. A range of other statutory regulatory bodies like the Health and Safety Executive had a hand in overseeing the performance of the NHS. There were also a wide range of other non-statutory regulators or inspectorates at work. In the 1980s the King's Fund had established an independent health care accreditation service modelled on those found in Canada and Australia and there were other accreditation or inspection bodies for service areas such as community hospitals and laboratory services (Scrivens 1995). The medical Royal Colleges undertook inspections of health care organisations to assess their ability to provide an adequate training environment for junior doctors. The NHS Litigation Authority set standards for risk management, and tested NHS organisations' performance against those standards. However, it would be difficult to argue that this mosaic of regulatory activities added up to a coherent, systematic and effective system of inspection or regulation for the NHS (Walshe 2003).

When the Labour government was elected in 1997, it turned to regulation to supplement its use of traditional mechanisms such as bureaucratic direction to direct the NHS, and announced in its first White Paper the creation of two new regulatory agencies – a National Institute of Clinical Excellence (NICE) tasked with providing national guidance and direction on clinical practice and technology assessment and a Commission for Health Improvement (CHI) with, in essence, the remit of a new NHS inspectorate (Department of Health 1997, 1998).

CHI was established in 1999, just after the statutory demise of HAS. There are some similarities in the genesis of the two organisations: both were created in response to a perceived crisis in the quality of NHS services; both were established by ministers who wanted them to be tough hospital inspectorates while civil servants and professionals wanted a more consensual and collaborative approach; and both began life with considerable political support and a high public profile. But there the similarities seem to end. HAS was set up at a time when inspection and regulation in public services were the exception rather than the rule, and public trust in the quality of services provided by the NHS was generally high. In contrast, CHI was created after regulation had already been extended to almost all areas of the public sector, and the largely unregulated NHS was starting to look like the exception. It came into being at a time when public faith in the NHS had been shaken by a series of very public failures in the quality of care (Walshe and Offen 2001). Perhaps most importantly, the remit of HAS was always restricted to areas such as long-term care for the elderly and mentally ill in which public and political interest was relatively low and the professions involved were fairly weak, while CHI was tasked with overseeing all

NHS organisations including the much more politically powerful and visible acute sector.

CHI was a non-departmental public body, like the Audit Commission, but was responsible to the Secretary of State at the Department of Health, who exercised considerable power and influence over the agency's work. CHI's board of commissioners were appointed by the Secretary of State, who also set the commission's annual budget and could direct it on what areas or issues it examines; and to whom its reports and recommendations were addressed. CHI had four main statutory functions which were laid down in the legislation:

- To undertake a rolling programme of four yearly clinical governance reviews of NHS organisations.

- To investigate serious service failures in the NHS when requested to do so by the Secretary of State or when asked to do so by others.

- To conduct national service reviews, which will monitor progress in the implementation of standards set by NICE, national service frameworks and, where required, other priorities.

- To provide advice and guidance to the NHS on clinical governance.

In addition, it was given a further responsibility in the NHS Plan (Department of Health 2000) for leading the collation and publication of performance assessment data on the NHS, in collaboration with the Department of Health and the Audit Commission.

CHI's responsibility for undertaking clinical governance reviews lay at the heart of its regulatory remit, and shaped its role as an inspectorate. Clinical governance was defined as 'a framework through which NHS organisations are accountable for continuously improving the quality of their services and safe-guarding high standards of care by creating an environment in which excellence in clinical care will flourish' (Department of Health 1998, p.33).

CHI's approach to establishing its expectations of clinical governance in NHS trusts was not to define a set of requirements in explicit standards and criteria, as many regulatory agencies do. While it set out quite clearly how the process of a clinical governance review was intended to work and the components of clinical governance which those reviews would examine, it chose not to define how each component should be measured, nor how the judgements reached by its review teams related to the evidence collected by the clinical governance review (CHI 2001), resulting in a review process which was less transparent and explicit than might be expected.

CHI reviews were undertaken by a multidisciplinary review team made up of around five reviewers, plus a CHI review manager, who co-ordinated the review, acted as the main liaison point between CHI and the NHS organisation, led and supported the review team during the visit itself, ensured that all the relevant evidence had been collected and documented, and wrote the report. Once an organisation was selected for a period review, CHI collected a wide range of data in advance to prepare its review team; scheduled and undertook a visit for the team of around five days to the organisation; and then produced a report, containing both descriptive narrative and explicit ratings of performance. The report identified key areas for action, and the organisation was required to produce and agree with CHI an action plan in response. The monitoring and implementation of that plan was the responsibility of the NHS organisations involved and the Department of Health, though CHI did undertake some follow-up work to its clinical governance reviews.

During its lifetime, CHI conducted over 378 clinical governance reviews of NHS organisations, investigated a series of serious failures in health services, undertook a number of national thematic studies, and took on responsibility for running the system of NHS performance ratings (commonly termed 'star ratings'). But in April 2002, just two years after CHI had been established, the government announced plans to reform health and social care regulation, bringing together the work of CHI in the NHS with the regulation of private health services in a new organisation to be called the Commission for Healthcare Audit and Inspection. These reforms are described below.

The history of regulation and inspection of non-NHS health services

Although most UK health care is provided by the NHS, there is a significant component both of private funding and private provision, especially in some sectors such as long-term care. Until relatively recently, the regulation of the private health care sector was, rather paradoxically, undertaken by the NHS. Health authorities (on behalf of the Secretary of State for Health) had statutory responsibilities under the Registered Homes Act 1984 and other legislation for regulating a wide range of health care providers – the title of the Act was somewhat misleading since it defined the organisations which came within its scope as follows:

- Any premises used or intended to be used for the reception of and provision of nursing for persons suffering from any sickness, injury or infirmity.

- Any premises used or intended to be used for the reception of pregnant women immediately after childbirth.

- Any other premises used for any or all of the following: carrying out of surgical procedures under anaesthesia; the termination of pregnancies; endoscopy; haemodialysis or peritoneal dialysis; or treatment by any 'specially controlled techniques' (a cover-all for things like laser cosmetic surgery, etc.).

This still left many health care providers almost wholly unregulated – from diagnostic services like pathology or radiology laboratories and health screening clinics to private drug and substance misuse clinics and domiciliary and daycare providers. Even for those which were regulated, the regulatory arrangements were widely regarded as somewhat unsatisfactory, for a number of reasons. First, the legislation was often criticised for giving health authorities little power to set standards of practice and placing upon them the responsibility for proving that health care provided was not adequate, rather than expecting the provider to show it was meeting the standards. While in theory health authorities had the power to sanction and ultimately delicence health care providers, in practice such sanctions were rarely used even in the face of continuing poor performance.

Second, the process was very fragmented, with every health authority running its own registration and inspection unit and often interpreting the standards very differently. For health care provider organisations which had multiple nursing homes or hospitals, there were considerable costs and problems associated with having to deal with multiple, different regulatory regimes. While some health authorities – particularly those with a substantial local private sector to regulate – did a good job, many gave their regulatory responsibilities a low priority, and evaluations suggested that most had serious flaws (Social Services Inspectorate 2001).

Third, the process was largely focused on premises and facilities, and did little to assure the quality and expertise of staff, or of processes of clinical care. Health authorities had few powers, for example, to concern themselves with the actual quality of clinical practice in private hospitals, and it was not unknown for clinicians removed from NHS organisations because of performance problems to resurface and continue to work unchecked in the private sector.

Fourth, and perhaps most importantly, the regulations had been drawn up at a time when the private health care sector was much smaller, and largely confined to non-acute services such as nursing home care, as the title of the legislation suggests. The growth of private health care in the UK over the 1980s and 1990s and the fragmented, outdated and incomplete systems of regulation meant that there was an overwhelming case for regulatory reform (Nazarko 1997).

The regulation of private health and social care was reformed in 2000 following a number of critical reports which highlighted the deficiencies and problems which have been outlined above (Burgner 1996; Health Select Committee 1999). A new national regulatory agency – NCSC – was established by the Care Standards Act 2000, and it formally assumed responsibility for regulating a wide range of health and social care providers in England from April 2002. It took over the work undertaken by 95 health authority registration and inspection units (which regulated nursing homes, independent hospitals, and other healthcare providers) and 150 local authority inspection units (which regulated care homes and some other social care providers.

The Commission was a non-departmental public body, accountable to the Secretary of State for Health to whom the Care Standards Act gave considerable power to direct NCSC's work programme. It was funded in part by registration fees charged to the organisations it regulated, and in part by the Department of Health. NCSC had four main functions: inspecting and regulating the health and social care providers who fall within its remit; improving the quality of services; supporting consumers by providing information and investigating complaints; and advising government on the quality of health and social care services. Its creation was intended to promote greater consistency and fairness through the application of one regulatory system across England, to bring greater independence and transparency to the regulatory process, to integrate health and social care regulation, and to extend regulatory protection to some areas which were not previously regulated at all (Hume 2001).

NCSC published the standards it used to regulate independent healthcare providers – acute hospitals, maternity services, psychiatric clinics, day surgery units, and so on (NCSC 2002). It set out 32 core standards, which applied to any organisation, and then further service-specific standards for different entities – 44 standards for acute hospitals, 47 for mental health establishments, 15 for hospices, 8 for maternity hospitals, and so on. The core standards dealt mainly with process-oriented generic issues, such as the provision of information to patients and systems for quality management, human resources, complaints, risk management and health records. The service specific standards were more clinically oriented – for example, the acute hospital standards included sections on children's services, surgery, critical care, radiology, pharmacy, pathology and cancer services.

The commission had a number of enforcement powers. First, its reports were published and it could use this mechanism to put non-compliance in the public domain and to pressure regulated organisations to comply. Second, it was able to take legal proceedings against regulated organisations that failed to comply with the regulations, which could result in a fine of up to £5000 either against the organisation or against individuals such as a nursing home manager or proprietor. Third, it was able to delicense both organisations and individuals, taking away an organisation's ability to provide regulated services, and preventing an individual from working in a management capacity in regulated organisations in the future.

Just a few weeks after NCSC formally assumed its regulatory responsibilities in April 2002, the government announced a wholesale reform of the regulation of both health and social care in England, which saw the functions of the commission divided between two new regulatory bodies – for health, and for social care. These changes are discussed in the next section.

Current regulatory arrangements for health services in England

In April 2002, just two years after the creation of the Commission for Health Improvement, and only two weeks after NCSC had taken over responsibility for regulating private health and social care, the Department of Health published proposals to rationalise health and social care regulation by creating two, new 'super-regulators' – a Commission for Healthcare Audit and Inspection, to regulate all health care provision, and a CSCI to regulate all social care. The Commission for Healthcare Audit and Inspection was to take over all the responsibilities of CHI; the private healthcare regulation function of NCSC; and the value for money audit function for the NHS of the Audit Commission;

as well as assuming some functions (like producing performance assessment statistics and star ratings) previously performed by the Department of Health. When in came into being, following primary legislation in 2003, the new body adopted the title of the Healthcare Commission (though its formal name in legislation remains the Commission for Healthcare Audit and Inspection).

These new regulatory arrangements need to be seen in the context of wider health policy changes and developments in England, which have increasingly emphasised the introduction of greater diversity and plurality in health care provision; the provision of greater choice of health services and providers for patients; and the creation of a 'self-improving' healthcare system in which central government, in the form of the Department of Health, plays a much more limited and focused role in policy development and oversight while others take responsibility for health care system management and delivery. So the government has encouraged private health care providers to enter the NHS market; has created new, more autonomous not-for-profit 'foundation NHS trusts' with defined memberships and elected boards of governors; and has looked increasingly to the voluntary or third sector to become engaged in service delivery. It has moved towards the creation of a national health system, funded largely through taxation but provided by a much more plural, diverse and market-oriented range of health care organisations. In that new environment, regulation and inspection play an increasingly important role in managing and directing the health care system.

The overall purpose of the Healthcare Commission is to promote improvements in health care and public health in England, and it has seven main statutory responsibilities, set out in the Health and Social Care (Community Health and Standards) Act 2003 and preceding legislation:

- To assess the management, provision and quality of NHS healthcare and public health services.

- To review the performance of each NHS trust and award an annual performance rating.

- To regulate the independent health care sector through registration, annual inspection, monitoring complaints and enforcement.

- To publish information about the state of health care.

- To consider complaints about NHS organisations that the organisations themselves have not resolved.

- To promote the co-ordination of reviews and assessments carried out by ourselves and others.

- To carry out investigations of serious failures in the provision of health care.

The Healthcare Commission is a non-departmental public body (like CHI and NCSC which it succeeded). Its board is appointed by the NHS Appointments Commission on behalf of the Department of Health, and its work is largely funded by a grant from the Department of Health though it does raise a proportion of its income from fees levied on private health care providers.

In the NHS, the Commission regulates around 582 NHS trusts (in primary care, acute, ambulance, mental health and learning disabilities) which, though they vary considerably in terms of their service areas and size/complexity, all function within the common context of the NHS. Most are essentially accountable to the Department of Health through strategic health authorities, though a small but growing number are foundation NHS trusts, more autonomous NHS bodies which are overseen by the independent regulator for NHS foundation trusts, Monitor. In the independent sector, the commission regulates around 1400 health care providers at present – which include independent treatment centres, private acute hospitals, mental health providers and private doctors. The numbers of regulated entities will grow rapidly when non-surgical cosmetic procedure providers are regulated.

The Healthcare Commission inherited two distinct and quite different regulatory regimes, which are described in Table 5.1. It is progressively harmonising its regulatory regime by, for example, moving in both sectors to the use of self-assessment supported by annual reviews and a proportionate and targeted programme of visits or inspections. The National Minimum Standards for independent health care and the Standards for Better Health for the NHS referred to in Table 5.1 differ both in structure and content. Arguably, the National Minimum Standards for independent health care impose a more explicit and demanding set of regulatory requirements in some respects. The commission has now organised its assessment processes in both sectors around the seven domains set out in Standards for Better Health (safety, clinical and cost effectiveness, governance, patient focus, accessible and responsive care, care environment and amenities, and public health) to create some consistency.

TABLE 5.1 THE REGULATORY REGIME OF THE HEALTHCARE
COMMISSION IN ENGLAND

	NHS health care providers	*Independent health care providers*
Direction	Department of Health produces Standards for Better Health, defining standards for NHS providers. Commission undertakes national reviews of National Service Frameworks and thematic areas.	Department of Health produces National Minimum Standards for independent health care providers, both generic and service specific (e.g. for mental health, acute, hospices, etc.).
Detection	Annual health check involves self-assessment and declaration by NHS organisations, linked by Commission to surveillance information/performance data, and resulting in an annual performance rating. Plans a programme of inspections/visits targeted using health check data, some of which will be unannounced.	Annual inspections of all independent health care providers (two-thirds announced, one-third unannounced). Providers complete a self-assessment first, which is used to focus the visit alongside other information. Inspections last two days, and a report is provided to the provider.
Enforcement	Publication of reports on and performance ratings of NHS organisations. Recommendations to Department of Health (for NHS trusts) and Monitor (for foundation trusts).	Report is published detailing findings and requirements (related to statutory regulations) and recommendations, and an action plan is required. Commission can take providers to court for non-compliance with requirements, seeking fines, and can deregister providers.

The commission has direct enforcement powers over independent health care providers, whom it can fine and ultimately delicense for non-compliance. However, its powers over NHS organisations are much more limited and are essentially exercised by making recommendations for action to the Department of Health or to Monitor (the regulator for NHS foundation trusts). One notable feature of the regulatory regime for both NHS and independent health care provision is that the Department of Health, rather than the Healthcare Commission, is responsible for setting the standards which the Commission then uses, or takes account of, in its regulatory interventions.

In April 2005, the Chancellor announced a wide-ranging reform of public services regulation and inspection in which the number of regulatory bodies was to be significantly reduced (see Chapters 1 and 10 for details). Among the changes he proposed was the amalgamation of the Healthcare Commission and CSCI. Subsequently, the Department of Health embarked on a regulatory review and consultation on the future purpose and function of health care regulation (Department of Health 2006). While the future structure and function of health care inspection and regulation remain to be determined, these latest changes are likely to continue the direction of policy travel for the last decade or more in England, in which government relies increasingly on a system of statutory regulation to oversee the performance of publicly funded health services, whether they are provided by public organisations or by not-for-profit or commercial private entities. While inspection will form a part of that regulatory regime, it is likely to encompass a wider range of regulatory functions and instruments including managing market entry and exit for providers, and setting or overseeing prices or charges.

The impact of regulation and inspection

The Healthcare Commission came into being relatively recently, and has already changed many aspects of the regulatory arrangements it inherited. There are no completed evaluations of the commission's impact available yet, though an evaluation of the annual health check is underway and a programme of research and evaluation is planned (Healthcare Commission 2006). Here, we therefore review evidence of the impact of past regulatory arrangements in the NHS and of health care regulation internationally.

A number of evaluations were undertaken of the work of CHI during its lifetime (Benson, Boyd and Walshe 2004, 2006; Day and Klein 2001, 2004;

NHS Confederation 2002, 2003; Walshe *et al.* 2001). While many of their findings concerned the process of review and how it was organised and perceived, their findings relating to impact are summarised in Table 5.2. Overall, the research suggests that CHI had some important impacts on the performance of NHS organisations through its clinical governance review

TABLE 5.2 THE IMPACT OF HEALTHCARE
REGULATION ON PERFORMANCE

Impact on structures	• Preparation and process of review onerous and time-consuming for the reviewed organisation, and diverted resources from other purposes.
	• Quality of the review/inspection team a crucial determinant of the overall value/impact of the review.
	• CHI reviews often led to important structural changes (to service management/leadership) and infrequently to major organisational changes/transitions.
Impact on processes	• Review process did not usually generate new knowledge about organisational performance but did make issues/problems explicit and cause them to be accorded greater priority by the organisation.
	• Most organisations report positively on the impact of the review process though a small number have negative experiences.
	• Concerns expressed about the lack of clear performance criteria for the review and the perceived ambiguity/lack of consistency in review judgements and findings.
	• Most CHI recommendations were focused on structures or processes of care, and were well accepted by organisations, and led to some change. However, action planning for change was often limited and follow-up by CHI and others was not systematic.
Impact on outcomes	• Very few CHI recommendations focused on service outcomes, and connections to outcomes were generally implicit in or assumed in recommendations which related to process.
	• Little evidence of changes in outcomes as a consequence of CHI reviews.

process, by catalysing change and shifting institutional dynamics to enable change to happen by according it greater priority or importance. However, it was difficult at a time of profound system-wide change in the NHS to point to measurable improvements resulting from CHI's regulatory oversight or to demonstrate causality. The CHI review process was continuously reviewed and updated in the light of experience, but still drew criticism for being too demanding in terms of data and resources, ambiguous about what was being measured and how/why, and lacking in consistency. Some aspects of CHI's regulatory regime were the product of its statutory remit and the pressures of the work programme set for it by the Department of Health.

The divergent development of regulation and inspection in health care in the four countries of the UK

Since the devolution of responsibility for health policy, including health system funding and management, to the Scottish Parliament and the National Assembly for Wales and the Northern Ireland Assembly, there has been a progressive divergence in policy priorities, structural arrangements and ways of working, which have in turn shaped the development of systems for inspection and regulation. While in England the Department of Health has pursued an increasing market-oriented health policy focused on choice and competition, with NHS service provision opened up to a wide range of new providers, in Scotland the Scottish Executive has abolished NHS trusts and created vertically integrated health boards combining acute, community and other health services. In Wales, there has been a strong focus on public health and linking the health service with local government boundaries and arrangements. In Northern Ireland, many features of the pre-1997 NHS have persisted because the suspension of the Assembly has made even limited reform difficult during an extended period of direct rule by the Northern Ireland Office. It can be argued that the NHS in England has moved furthest from the traditional, public bureaucracy model for organising the NHS.

Before devolution, CHI worked across the NHS in England and Wales, while the Scottish NHS had its own separate arrangements for the oversight of NHS performance based around the Clinical Standards Board for Scotland, the Clinical Resource and Audit Group, the Health Technology Board for Scotland and other bodies. Since devolution, each country has put its own regulation and inspection arrangements in place. Those for England have already been reviewed above.

In Scotland, NHS Quality Improvement Scotland (QIS) was established as a special health board in 2003 to bring together work on quality and performance in the Scottish NHS which was previously undertaken by a number of separate organisations and initiatives. QIS has a wide range of responsibilities including: providing advice and guidance to the NHS in Scotland on clinical practice; setting clinical and non-clinical standards of care and targets for performance; assessing the performance of the 11 health boards against those standards and reporting in public on the results; investigating serious service failures; and supporting the development of quality improvement through programmes, project and initiatives. The role, function and approach of QIS reflect the much more integrated nature of the NHS and its direct management by the Scottish Executive and close oversight by the Scottish Parliament. Independent health care providers in Scotland are regulated by the Scottish Commission for the Regulation of Care (known as the Care Commission, which is the regulator for social care services) rather than by QIS.

In Wales, the Commission for Health Improvement was replaced in 2004 with a new body, titled the Health Inspectorate Wales (HIW), with a remit to inspect and investigate health service and to report to the Assembly via the health and social care directorate. It is, like other National Assembly for Wales inspectorates, operationally independent of government, and will inspect NHS organisations against a set of standards produced by an Assembly group called the Advisory Board for Healthcare Standards in Wales. From 2006, HIW assumed responsibility for inspecting and regulating private and independent health care providers in Wales.

In Northern Ireland, a new regulator for both health and social care, the Regulation and Quality Improvement Authority (RQIA), came into being in 2005. It has responsibility for regulating all health and social care provision by both the health and social services boards (which provide integrated NHS health and social care service) and by private and independent organisations including private hospitals, nursing and residential homes, children's homes, nursing and medical staff agencies, and other entities. RQIA is still engaged in establishing its structures and systems for inspection and regulation.

The future for health care inspection

There has been a tremendous growth in the use of systems of inspection or regulation in health care in the UK over the last two decades, and at the same time those systems and the agencies responsible for regulation and inspection have been repeatedly reorganised. While the rapid pace of reform in regulation in some ways simply reflects the rate of change in the National Health Service and the wider health care system, it also means that there is a fragmented and complex history from which it is not straightforward to draw clear and coherent conclusions. It has been almost impossible to undertake the crucial task of evaluating the work of regulatory agencies like the Commission for Health Improvement, understanding their impact on the performance of health care organisations and the quality of service provided to patients, and using that knowledge both to learn about the business of inspection and regulation and to improve the regulatory regime in health care. In its short four-year life, CHI developed and revised its methods for clinical governance reviews, investigations and national studies; faced considerable political pressure to be more combative and aggressive in its approach to inspection; suffered repeated demands from government that it should take on a range of new tasks and roles; and barely managed to complete its first round of inspections of NHS trusts by the time it was replaced by the Healthcare Commission. That organisation is, in turn, subject to a proposed reorganisation as it merges with the CSCI in 2008 or 2009. An obvious but important lesson for policymakers is that establishing an effective set of regulatory arrangements takes time, and repeated revisions of the policy objectives and purposes of regulation makes effective regulation more difficult and less likely.

The future for health care inspection and regulation in the four countries of the UK seems likely to continue to diverge. In Wales and Scotland, where government has shown a continuing commitment to a near public monopoly of health service funding and provision, it seems likely that the regulatory authorities will continue to act largely as a traditional public service inspectorate, working for and with government to oversee the performance of public agencies which run health services. In England, where a much more diverse, plural and competitive health care economy is emerging, the regulatory mission seems likely to be both more complex and more central to the working of a market-based health care system.

References

Allsop, J. and Saks, M. (2003) *Regulating the Health Professions.* London: Sage.

Benson, L.A., Boyd, A. and Walshe, K. (2004) *Learning from CHI: The Impact of Healthcare Regulation.* Manchester: MCHM.

Benson, L.A., Boyd, A. and Walshe, K. (2006) 'Learning from regulatory interventions in healthcare: The Commission For Health Improvement and its clinical governance review process.' *Clinical Governance: An International Journal 11,* 3, 213–224.

Burgner, T. (1996) *The Regulation and Inspection of Social Services.* London: Department of Health/Welsh Office.

Commission for Health Improvement (CHI) (2001) *A Guide to Clinical Governance Reviews in NHS Acute Trusts.* London: CHI.

Crossman, R. (1977) *The Diaries of a Cabinet Minister, Vol III.* London: Hamilton Cape.

Day, P., Klein, R. and Tipping, G. (1988) *Inspecting for Quality: Services for the Elderly.* Bath: Centre for the Analysis of Social Policy, University of Bath.

Day, P. and Klein, R. (2001) *Auditing the Auditors: Audit in the National Health Service.* London: The Stationery Office/Nuffield Trust.

Day, P. and Klein, R. (2004) *The NHS Improvers: A Study of the Commission for Health Improvement.* London: King's Fund.

Department of Health (1997) *The New NHS: Modern, Dependable.* London: Department of Health.

Department of Health (1998) *A First Class Service: Quality in the New NHS.* London: Department of Health.

Department of Health (2000) *The NHS Plan: A Plan for Investment, A Plan for Reform.* London: The Stationery Office.

Department of Health (2006) *The Future Regulation of Health and Adult Social Care in England.* London: Department of Health.

Department of Health and Social Security (1969) *Report of the Committee of Inquiry into Allegations of Ill-treatment of Patients and other Irregularities at the Ely Hospital, Cardiff.* London: HMSO.

Greer, S. (2005) 'The politics of health policy divergence.' *Regional and Federal Studies 15,* 4, 501–518.

Healthcare Commission (2006) *Evaluating the Activities of the Healthcare Commission.* London: Healthcare Commission.

Health Select Committee (1999) *Fifth Report: The Regulation of Private and Other Independent Healthcare.* London: The Stationery Office.

Henkel, M., Kogan, M., Packwood, T., Whitaker, T. and Youll, P. (1989) *The Health Advisory Service: An Evaluation.* London: King's Fund.

Hume, C. (2001) 'The National Care Standards Commission; what it means for nurses.' *Nursing Standard 8,* 5, 8–10.

National Care Standards Commission (NCSC) (2002) *Independent Health Care: National Minimum Standards Regulations.* London: The Stationery Office.

Nazarko, L. (1997) 'A question of inspection.' *Nursing Times 93,* 46, 40–42.

NHS Confederation (2002) *Reviewing the Reviewers: NHS Experience of CHI Clinical Governance Reviews.* London: NHS Confederation.

NHS Confederation (2003) *Re-reviewing the Reviewers: A Second Survey of NHS Trust Experience of CHI Clinical Governance Reviews.* London: NHS Confederation.

Scrivens, E. (1995) *Accreditation: Protecting the Professional or the Consumer?* Maidenhead: Open University Press.

Social Services Inspectorate (2001) *Safe Enough? Inspection of Health Authority Registration and Inspection Units 2000.* London: Department of Health.

Walshe, K. (2003) *Regulating Healthcare: A Prescription for Improvement?* Maidenhead: Open University Press.

Walshe, K. and Offen, N. (2001) 'A very public failure: Lessons for quality improvement in healthcare organisations from the Bristol Royal Infirmary.' *Quality in Health Care 10,* 250–256.

Walshe, K., Wallace, L., Latham, L., Freeman, T. and Spurgeon, P. (2001) 'The external review of quality improvement in healthcare organisations: A qualitative study.' *International Journal of Quality in Health Care 13,* 5, 367–374.

CHAPTER 6

Inspection and the Criminal Justice Agencies

John W. Raine

Introduction

In November 2005, the UK government published a Policy Statement (OCJR 2005) setting out its proposals for reforming the inspection arrangements for criminal justice in England and Wales. These centred on the creation of a single new Inspectorate for Justice, Community Safety and Custody to be achieved by bringing together the existing five separate inspectorates – for police, prosecution, courts administration, probation and prisons respectively.

Realisation of these proposals and the establishment of the new single inspectorate seemed, at the time, highly probable, since there was at least tacit support from within several of the chief inspectors in post. However, the passage of the proposals through parliament, as part of the Police and Justice Bill, proved less straightforward and on 10 October 2006 the government saw it necessary to table a series of amendments to the Bill, immediately before its third reading in the House of Lords, which in effect put pay to the merger proposals. This followed a heated debate in the House of Lords, in which the former Chief Inspector of Prisons, Lord Ramsbotham, led a particularly vigorous challenge, and with the Minister responsible for Criminal Justice and Offender Management, the Rt Hon Baroness Scotland of Asthal QC, seeming to be the only protagonist.

Immediately after the debate, the Home Secretary, the Lord Chancellor and the Attorney General – the triumvirate of ministers responsible for criminal justice in England and Wales – released an exchange of letters they had had with the chief inspectors of the five inspectorates in which they stated:

> We have recognised the serious concerns about aspects of our proposals and agree with you that the focus of our effort should now be on finding ways to strengthen and improve joint working rather than on proposals for organisational merger. (*Guardian*, 19 October 2006, p.14)

In this chapter we explore the arguments behind the government's defeat and backtrack on the proposal for a single 'Inspectorate for Justice, Community Safety and Custody'. We begin by summarising the existing framework for inspection within criminal (and civil) justice. We then proceed to outline and examine the contribution that inspection agencies have made and their impacts on the different functional responsibilities in the sector, before examining the arguments for and against the change to a single inspectorate. Finally, we consider how some of the arguments, especially around the inspection of our prisons, cast doubt on the merit of the government's proposals and generated fresh debate about the purposes of inspection and concern that the kinds of managerial values and purposes that increasingly dominate inspectorial processes should not trump other considerations.

The existing inspection framework in criminal justice

In recent years the criminal justice sector in England and Wales has been subject to inspection by five separate service-oriented inspectorates, each established by statute as independent from, albeit 'hosted' by, a government department and with the chief inspectors being royal appointments. An equivalent but separate set of five inspectorates undertake the same functions in Scotland, although in Northern Ireland, in some contrast, much the same responsibilities lie with a single inspectorate (Criminal Justice Inspection Northern Ireland). The five inspectorates for England and Wales are: HM Inspectorate of Constabulary (HMIC); HM Crown Prosecution Service Inspectorate; HM Inspectorate of Court Administration (HMICA); HM Inspectorate of Probation; and HM Inspectorate of Prisons. The first of these is the longest established – having been created in 1856, while the Crown Prosecution Service Inspectorate and that for Court Administration are comparatively recent arrivals to the inspectorial genre – dating back to just 2000 and 2003 respectively – as such having been created by the same New Labour administration that in 2005–06 was seeking to rationalise inspection services. The histories of HM Inspectorates of Prisons and of Probation date back to the 1830s and 1930s respectively, although in their current statutory form they are both comparatively recent institutional developments.

Although these five inspectorates largely align with the five principal public sector criminal justice agencies – of the Police, Crown Prosecution Service, the Courts, the Probation Service and the Prison Service – in detail, some of the responsibilities extend beyond the criminal justice sector and include oversight of civil and family justice as well. HMI Prisons, for example, also has responsibility for inspecting immigration removal centres (and the associated short-term holding centres and escorts), while HMICA inspects the administration of the civil and family courts as well as those for criminal matters. Similarly, the responsibilities of HMIC extend to include inspection of some specialised policing operations, notably British Transport Police, the Civil Nuclear Constabulary and the Ministry of Defence Police and the new Serious Organised Crime Agency.

HM Inspectorate of Constabulary

Since its formation more than one and a half centuries ago, HMIC has been charged with examining and improving the efficiency of the Police Service in England and Wales (as indicated, Scotland has its own HMIC, while in Northern Ireland the single criminal justice inspectorate undertakes the equivalent responsibilities). While it is all too easy today to imagine that governmental concern with public service efficiency in Britain largely began when Mrs Thatcher became Prime Minister in 1979, the wording of Section 15 of the County and Borough Police Act of 1856 (reproduced below) had at its very core the idea that every county and borough should maintain an efficient police force, that forces would be inspected annually by the newly created Inspectorate of Constabulary, and indeed that payment of a 25 per cent central government grant towards local policing costs would be contingent on the inspectors finding local forces to be performing efficiently:

> It shall be lawful for Her Majesty, by Warrant under Her Royal Sign Manual, to appoint during Her Majesty's Pleasure Three Persons as Inspectors under this Act, to visit and inquire into the State and the Efficiency of the Police appointed for every County and Borough, and whether the Provisions of the Acts under which such Police are appointed are duly

observed and carried into effect, and also into the State of the Police Stations, Charge Rooms, Cells or Lock-ups, or other Premises occupied for the Use of such Police. (County and Borough Police Act 1856, Section 15)

Although the 1856 Act did not provide a very specific definition of efficiency, the legislation set out conditions for issuing the certificates of efficiency: the size of the police force; the ratio of numbers of officers to the local population size; the quality of supervision exercised over the constables; and the degree of co-operation given to neighbouring forces. All four criteria still have a resonance 150 years later, and the fourth – about cross-boundary collaboration – seems particularly interesting when set alongside the recent controversy about police force amalgamations in England and Wales.

The very first inspector's report was published in autumn 1857 and, not unlike those of more recent years, highlighted significant variations between forces (Crowley and Todd 2006a, p.17). While of the county forces only Rutland was officially deemed to be 'inefficient' in this initial survey, the position in the borough forces was generally viewed as much more problematical, both in terms of the inadequacy of force size and indiscipline. In some contrast with the contemporary situation, the early inspectors' findings seemed to invoke little apparent concern on the part of the Home Secretary and his undersecretaries at the Home Office. Here the prevailing view was of policing as a local government matter. As a result, little central effort was devoted to co-ordinating the inspectors' activities or to developing national policy or setting policing standards.

Gradually this viewpoint changed, of course, and the Police Act 1964 introduced the basis for the current 'tripartite governance framework' – of Home Secretary, Police Authority and Chief Constable, each with responsibilities in relation to policing policy and practice. The 1960s also saw the appointment of the first Chief Inspector of Constabulary for England and Wales – replacing the previous arrangement of local inspectors each visiting forces within separate areas. From then on, of course, the centrally driven pursuit of efficiency and effectiveness in policing has been relentless. Here the work of the inspectorate has been increasingly defined by government through, for example, the development of the legal requirements on police authorities to provide Best Value for taxpayers, and to conduct Best Value Reviews of aspects of police force activity to be monitored and assessed by the inspectorate (Hale, Heaton and Uglow 2004). Similarly the inspectorate, as a key user, has been closely involved in the development of performance monitoring tools – first the set of Best Value Performance Indicators (BVPIs) and, subsequently, a more sophisticated system for monitoring policing performance – the Policing Performance Assessment Framework (PPAF).

Overall, it is undoubtedly in the area of managerial performance where the contribution of HMIC has been most significant and where the agency has had most impact. Although government itself has increasingly provided much of the challenge for police forces to improve their detection rates, and performance in crime reduction through the setting and close monitoring of national targets, and through sharpening the whole basis of accountability in policing, the inspectorate's work has been very important in this context too. Indeed, it has often been HMIC reports that have been key to government's ability to shape the policing policy agenda; for example, most recently in relation to the strengthening of police capability for 'public protection' (and which underpinned the government's interest in force amalgamations in 2006).

HM Inspectorate of Court Administration

As indicated above, HMICA is a comparatively recent addition to the inspectorate family. The current organisational structure was created in 2005 under powers established in the Courts Act 2003. However, prior to this an inspectorate for magistrates' courts (HM Magistrates' Courts Service Inspectorate) had existed since 1993. The remit of the new organisation was to inspect the administration of the Crown, county and magistrates' courts of England and Wales, and also the Children and Family Court Advisory and Support Service.

Particularly significant in this context is the limit placed on the inspectors' remit to matters of court administration – the inspectors being constrained by the legislation from inspecting 'persons making judicial decisions or exercising judicial discretion'. This limitation aims, of course, to respect the constitutional requirement of judicial independence, although in practice it is rarely straightforward to distinguish precisely within a courts' context between administrative and judicial responsibility insofar as each interrelates with the other. The limitation also inevitably lessens the potential interest of the general public in the work of this inspectorate, although there has been a strong focus on inspecting the quality of service at the courts, a matter of high relevance at least to some groups – victims, witnesses, defendants, appellants, and so on. Arguably, the main impacts of the inspectorate have been in relation to the raising of standards of service – both court accommodation and professionalism in court administration – and particularly in promoting greater uniformity across the country in the quality of service offered, as well as addressing administrative inefficiency and delays in hearing cases.

Her Majesty's Crown Prosecution Service Inspectorate

HMCPSI is a similarly recent creation, having been formed in October 2000 to provide an independent inspectorate for the Crown Prosecution Service – the principal prosecuting authority for criminal cases in England and Wales. The purpose of this inspectorate, like HMICA, is defined very much in the contemporary managerial and regulatory parlance as being:

> to promote continuous improvement in the efficiency, effectiveness and fairness of the prosecution services within a joined-up criminal justice system through the process of inspection, evaluation and identification of good practice. (HMCPSI Annual Report 2004–05, p.11)

This purpose has led the inspectorate to focus upon the following key themes: the quality of pre-charge decision-making, caseload management, achieving successful outcomes in cases (i.e. successfully prosecuting the cases and reducing the proportion of cases that fail during the process and are not prosecuted as planned (e.g. because of witnesses failing to attend court), the handling of sensitive cases, compliance with the statutory time limits of holding suspects in custody, quality of service to victims and witnesses, quality of presentation of cases in court, and resource and performance management within the CPS.

As with HMICA, the public profile of this inspectorate has to date been quite low, partly a reflection of its short lifespan to date, but perhaps particularly because its dominant focus has been on an essentially internally oriented agenda of managerial performance, as opposed to the more sensitive policy considerations that from time to time arise in relation to decisions to prosecute (or not) cases of high public interest. Accordingly, its main impacts have tended to be focused on improving and standardising managerial processes and performance efficiency across the country.

HM Inspectorate of Probation

The history, if not the public profile, of HM Inspectorate of Probation goes back rather further to 1936 and the recommendations of a Departmental

Committee Report on the work of social services in the Courts of Summary Jurisdiction. Initially, its remit focused on inspecting local probation areas and the quality of training of probation staff. It was also accorded a formal role in confirming the appointment of all probation officers, which resulted in the need for a number of regional offices around the country, most of which continued to operate until the 1980s.

In Scotland, inspection of probation work continued to reflect the traditional links between probation and social work with the work being undertaken by the Social Work Inspection Agency. South of the border in England and Wales, however, a Government Efficiency Scrutiny study resulted in significant changes being made in 1987 to the structure and working methods of the inspectorate. These included the transfer of its training functions to a number of higher education establishments. At the same time, the focus of the inspectorate's work was redefined towards the assessment of the effectiveness of probation provision in each of the local probation areas. Four years later, under the Criminal Justice Act 1991, the work of the inspectorate was placed on a statutory footing and the agency was accorded equal status to the other criminal justice inspectorates. Its role was further refined in 2000 when local probation services were nationalised under the new National Probation Department (NPD). The inspectorate's title was accordingly revised (extended) to Her Majesty's Inspectorate of the National Probation Service for England and Wales, and new powers were vested in the Secretary of State to appoint inspectors to undertake inspections and to report to him on youth offending work as a whole, as well as on probation specifically. As such, the inspectorate has increasingly developed its reputation in the criminal justice sector for its independent-minded review work on some sensitive issues such as early release of prisoners into the community, probation hostels and drug treatments, in addition to the more routine task of assessing the effectiveness and efficiency of probation work around the country.

HM Inspectorate of Prisons

In certain key respects, the remit of the Prisons Inspectorate for England and Wales (and in Scotland also) contrasts quite markedly with each of the inspectorates discussed above. Although established in its current form only a comparatively short time before the inspectorates for court administration and prosecution, the origins of the Prisons Inspectorate reach back to 1835 when the first inspectors were appointed. In 1878 inspection became an internal function of the Prison Commission, and later of the Prison Department. However, the argument for an independent inspectorate, outside the civil service, came to prominence again in the 1960s and, although remaining an internal function of government for another two decades, the appointment in 1967 of Brigadier Maunsel as Inspector General by Home Secretary, Roy Jenkins, following the Mountbatten Report, set the inspectorate on its course towards independence (Morgan 1985). This was finally achieved in 1982, following the May Report, and even though this was a time when the new managerial values of the Thatcher administration were beginning to take a grip in the public sector, the particular priorities and purposes established for the new independent Prisons Inspectorate for England and Wales were defined quite differently and specifically focused on reporting on conditions for and treatment of those in prison, young offender institutions and immigration removal centres.[1]

From this formative time onwards, successive chief inspectors of prisons have been appointed from outside the Prison Service, and for terms of just five years, to report directly to the Home Secretary, and on any matters relating to the remit that they feel require attention. Although they will always be supported by a team of staff with direct experience from within the Prison Service (and at various levels of seniority), and also by Home Office officials and by other specialist experts as required, the concept of the chief inspector approaching the task in a very personal manner and essentially conducting the inspection from a lay perspective has been a notable characteristic of this particular inspectorate from the outset. Reports from the chief inspector on the conditions and regimes operative in women's prisons, and indeed in young offenders' institutions, have been particularly influential in leading to significant raising of standards. As a former Chief Inspector, Judge Stephen Tumim has pointed out that this has particular advantages. If one is not inspecting the work and outcomes of former professional colleagues, or visiting institutions with which there is strong familiarity, it follows that 'the Service knows it cannot respond to criticism with the equivalent of the comment

---

1   Although the statutory remit of the chief inspector covers England and Wales, by invitation, the inspector may also inspect prisons in Northern Ireland, the Channel Islands, Isle of Man and some Commonwealth dependent territories. Scotland has its own Prisons Inspectorate.

"well we have always done it this way" and expect it to be accepted' (Tumim 1992, p.5).

Compared with the other inspectorates, the brief of the Chief Inspector of Prisons is much more akin to that of the independent consultant on prison conditions, and much less focused on managerial performance other than in terms of the ways in which this impinges upon the treatment of prisoners. In this regard, of course, the main unit of inspection is individual prisons and the activities and regimes taking place within them, rather than on management across a larger territorial area, such as a police force or probation area. That said, as with the other inspectorates, most of the work of the Prisons Inspectorate takes the form of an annual programme of routine inspections, with the expectation that all prisons in England and Wales will be visited at regular intervals. As indicated, particular attention is paid to the standards of accommodation for, and treatment of, prisoners, and the general conditions inside the jails. The inspections also often result in reports on the contribution that prisons make to public protection and to reducing reoffending (e.g. through providing effective and constructive forms of training and education for inmates and by preparing them for release) and, as indicated, will mainly consider efficiency and other organisational performance and resource management issues in the context of their impacts on the quality of the prison regimes.

In both its remit and approach to its work, the Prisons Inspectorate, far more than the other inspectorates, demonstrates the spirit of 'public accountability' and indeed the contribution of successive chief inspectors of prisons has been noteworthy for the succession of critical reports about inadequate facilities, poor treatment of prisoners and shortcomings in the regimes more generally, which are routinely profiled by the media, thus placing the issues of prison conditions strongly in the public eye and consciousness. Indeed, like her predecessors, Judge Stephen Tumim and Sir David Ramsbotham, the current Chief Inspector, Anne Owers, has a relatively high public and media profile – certainly in comparison with their counterparts in prosecution, probation, court administration and police inspection.

Largely, of course, this reflects the high public interest in penal affairs, in the details of the regimes and facilities for those in custody, in what is done with regard to rehabilitation and in relation to respect for human rights. Moreover, the media profiling of critical inspection reports has inevitably often made for difficult relationships between the chief inspector and government ministers, particularly if the findings are at odds with government policy or because they expose either undue political interference or managerial incompetence in the running of the prisons. In this regard, the stewardship of Sir David Ramsbotham as chief inspector was particularly marked by some strained relations with Home Secretary Michael Howard.

A single inspectorate for justice, community safety and custody?

So why in 2005 did the government propose to change the inspectorial arrangements in favour of a single inspectorate, and in so doing backtrack on arrangements that had only recently been put in place or revised? The main reason undoubtedly lay outside criminal justice and in the wider arena of debate about the nature of regulation and inspection in this country – about which, of course, this volume as a whole is concerned. Certainly this is how the proposals for a single Inspectorate for Justice, Community Safety and Custody were framed and presented. As such, they could be seen not just as an element of the government's ambitions to create a more focused and joined up justice system but along with other reformed inspectorial regimes as a key component of the wider New Labour vision for a modernised and efficient public sector. The earlier establishment of a single criminal justice inspectorate in Northern Ireland probably also added impetus to the commitment to achieve such a vision within England and Wales.

As discussed elsewhere in this volume, a policy paper on regulatory and inspectorial functions (Office for Public Service Reform 2003) set the agenda for the rationalisation and joining up of criminal justice inspection. The basic principles for inspection as laid out in that document were generally welcomed within criminal justice, not least because they implied that the unequivocal priorities for inspection should be service improvement and the attainment of better outcomes for users. The proposed merger of the inspectorates was also, the government argued, intended to give greater emphasis to user focus and make inspection less burdensome to inspected bodies.

The Policy Statement published in November 2006 on the proposals for a single inspectorate for 'Justice and Community Safety' – at that stage the proposed title excluded specific reference to 'custody' – (Home Office 2006) highlighted in its title the government's desire to push inspection within the criminal justice context more in the direction of 'community safety' – as indeed was the case with crime and criminal justice policy more generally, with more and more emphasis being placed on antisocial behaviour, on 'fear of crime' and on building greater confidence in law and order on the streets.

Reactions to these proposals were mixed. Supporters of the principle of a single inspectorate saw the opportunity for inspection to become more joined up, as with the Northern Ireland Inspection Service. In her research on inspectorates across the public services, Mordaunt (2000), for example, noted strong support for better joint working from the Chief Inspector of Probation, based on his first-hand experience of the benefits of joint inspectorial worked with HMIC (on crime prevention) and with HMI Prisons (on the rehabilitation of offenders into the community).

However, critics raised concerns about the loss of specialist service expertise that was felt to be an inevitable consequence if a single Inspectorate for England and Wales were to span policing and prosecution, the courts, and the probation and prison services as well. There was significant disquiet about the implications for the Prison Service, the inspectorate for which, as we have seen, was established for distinctly different purposes than the other inspectorates. As Faulkner (2006, p.2) reminded in his submission in response to the government's consultation on the single inspectorate:

> The Inspectorates of Prisons and Probation are the principal means by which society can ensure that those punished by the courts, and especially those held in closed institutions, are treated in accordance with civilised standards of decency, humanity and human rights. Her Majesty's Inspectorate of Prisons was created in its present form precisely because the function was not being performed adequately or convincingly by the internal inspectorate which had existed previously. It is independent of the Prison Service, as recognised in its title; its functions and powers are defined in statute; the Chief Inspector reports directly to Ministers; the Inspectorate is not bound by the procedures of the Prison Service; and in reporting to Ministers it will recognise but it is not limited by the constraints which apply to the Service itself... It contributes to the efficiency of the Service and to the achievement of its objectives, but it does not exist for that purpose.

In the event such concerns and criticisms hardly seemed to move the government and when the final Policy Statement was published in November

2005, and the relevant clauses were subsequently written into the Police and Justice Bill, there seemed little in the way of concessions beyond the addition of the words 'and Custody' on the end of the proposed title for the new inspectorate – an olive branch of recognition of the arguments and a tacit acceptance of the special responsibilities that a single inspectorate would have to undertake in relation to prisons. But it was to no effect. As explained, when the time came for the clauses to be debated in the House of Lords, the proposals were subjected to a withering attack led by former Prisons Inspector Lord Ramsbotham, and with the long list of opponents also including 11 Labour peers, including a former Prisons Minister.

Conclusions

More than anything the failure of the project to establish a single Inspectorate for Justice, Community Safety and Custody hinged on differences of view as to the purposes of inspection and doubts about the capacity of one organisation to give due attention to such differences. The past 10 to 15 years have, of course, been a period in which managerialist values have been relentlessly expressed, on the one hand, in the preoccupation with indicator-and-target-driven performance management, and on the other, with the constant revision of organisational structures and processes. To a large extent the government's proposals for a single inspectorate were predicated on those values and priorities. But the Prison Service, in particular, had existed from the outset to reflect different purposes and values – 'theta' values of fairness and a concern for people and process and 'lambda' values of standards of safety and personal security, rather than 'sigma' values of economy and parsimony in resource use so strongly associated with the New Public Management (Hood 1991).

Above all, the proposals for merger into a single inspectorate failed because they could not command sufficient confidence that one organisation could effectively fulfil the different inspection purposes and reflect such different value systems. Although in this instance unsuccessfully opposed, criticisms of the plans announced two years earlier to create a single correctional services agency – the National Offender Management Service (NOMS), drawing probation and prison management together – were based on much the same grounds.

Here we come up against the fundamental issue that, although 'interdependence' and (in the modern-day parlance) 'joined-up' approaches have both reality and importance in the strategic direction and everyday world of criminal justice in ensuring greater clarity, comprehensibility and certainty for users, and for helping to ensure overall system efficiency, equally important in our constitutional framework is the notion of 'independence' and respect for the separate purposes, tasks and conditions involved in responding to crime. While this is most evident in relation to the vital constitutional imperative of the separation of powers and the independence of the judiciary, in many respects the issue goes further. It was, for example, at the heart of the reasoning for the creation of the Crown Prosecution Service in 1985 that there should be organisational separation and independence between the investigatory and prosecuting functions (both hitherto having been policing responsibilities).

A key challenge in criminal justice is of course to achieve an appropriate balance between independence and interdependence (Raine and Willson 1993) and to that end, the agreement hurriedly brokered between the government and the chief inspectors, shortly after the House of Lords defeat, to pursue more joint working between the inspectorates, was the probably best possible outcome. Certainly it suggests that inspection in criminal justice can continue to develop specialist service expertise and understanding and in this way best support and prompt the respective agencies towards better outcomes, while also facilitating the important project of making criminal justice collectively work more effectively for everyone's benefit.

Most important, the model of 'more joint working between separate inspectorates' in England and Wales promises to promote more learning about the role and process of inspection as the separate inspectorates both innovate and develop for their own purposes and as they exchange their ideas and experiences for the benefit of all (Grace 2005). Such benefits have already begun to be realised through the increased amount of joint inspection work that has been undertaken in recent years and where the experiences have generally been extremely positive (see, for example, HM Inspectorates of Probation and Constabulary 2005; HM Inspectorates 2006; HM Inspectorate of Probation 2006; Home Office 1999; Morgan 2004).

Key also in this context of learning and development is the issue of the inspectorates' role in relation to accountability, and particularly the balance that is struck between *managerial accountability* on the one hand and *public accountability* on the other (Raine, Dunstan and Patrick 2006). As indicated, for the most part, at least in recent years, inspection work has mainly seemed to focus on the former – and has been particularly concerned to check how well the organisations are doing against the various targets and expectations set for, and often by, their management. Mainly the focus here has been on an 'internal' performance management agenda of efficiency and effectiveness, and of 'ticking the boxes' in terms of corporate organisational leadership agendas and such like. It is perhaps no surprise that the inspectorates for court administration, probation, prisons, and to some extent police as well, have generally had a relatively low public profile, with their reports rarely attracting national media interest. As we have seen, however, with the Inspectorate for Prisons, on the other hand, the emphasis from the outset has been much more on public accountability, and with much stronger media profiling and lively public interest in the findings and conclusions of the reports from the chief inspector.

Arguably, the most convincing case for the added public sector bureaucracy and cost of inspection – in whatever context – is the capacity it creates for enhancing *public accountability* through the provision of independent, authoritative and rounded assessments for ministers and the public at large of the strengths and shortcomings of our public services (Hartley 1972; Hood *et al.* 1999; Power 1997). The survival, at least for the time being, of the five inspectorates of criminal justice in England and Wales provides an opportunity to reflect more deeply on the possibility that inspection in criminal justice might in future take its lead more strongly from the prisons' example and at least balance the concern to scrutinise managerial performance – through the plethora of indicators, attainment of targets and performance in league tables, etc. – with more focus on the role in terms of public accountability and the associated provision of information for public debate and judgement.

References

Crowley, R. and Todd, P. (2006a) *The History of Her Majesty's Inspectorate of Constabulary: The First 100 Years.* London: HMIC.
Crowley, R. and Todd, P. (2006b) *The History of Her Majesty's Inspectorate of Constabulary: The Modern Inspectorate.* London: HMIC.
Faulkner, D. (2006) Response to the Home Office Consultation on 'A Single Inspectorate for Justice and Community Safety'. London: Home Office.
Grace, C. (2005) 'Change and improvement in audit and inspection: A strategic approach for the 21st Century.' *Local Government Studies 31,* 5, 575–596.
Guardian Newspaper (2006) Justice inspectorate plans to be abandoned, 19 October 2006, p.14.

Hale, C., Heaton, R. and Uglow, S. (2004) 'Uniform styles? Aspects of police centralisation in England and Wales.' *Policing and Society 14*, 4, 291–312.

Hartley, O. A. (1972) 'Inspectorates in British Central Government.' *Public Administration 49*, 439–456.

HM Inspectorate of Probation (2006) *Joint Thematic Inspection Report: Putting Risk of Harm in Context: An Inspection Promoting Public Protection*. London: Home Office.

HMCPSI (2005) *HM Chief Inspector's Annual Report 2004–05*, HC 129. London: The Stationery Office.

HM Inspectorates (2006) *Joint Inspection Report: Thames Valley Criminal Justice Area*. London: Home Office.

HM Inspectorates of Probation and Constabulary (2005) *Managing Sex Offenders in the Community: A Joint Inspection*. London: HMIP and HMIC.

Home Office (1999) *Lifers: A Joint Thematic Review by Her Majesty's Inspectorates of Prisons and Probation*. London: Home Office.

Home Office (2006) *A Single Inspectorate for Justice and Community Safety*. London: Home Office.

Hood, C. (1991) 'A public management for all seasons?' *Public Administration 69*, 1, 69–82.

Hood, C., Scott, C., James, O., Jones, G. and Travers, T. (1999) *Regulation Inside Government*. Oxford: Oxford University Press.

Mordaunt, E. (2000) 'The emergence of multi-inspectorate inspections: "Going it alone is not an option".' *Public Administration 78*, 4, 751–769.

Morgan, R. (1985) 'Her Majesty's Inspectorate of Prisons.' In M. Maguire, J. Vagg and R. Morgan, *Accountability and Prisons: Opening Up a Closed World*. London: Tavistock.

Morgan, R. (2004) 'Thinking about the future of probation inspection.' *Howard Journal of Criminal Justice 43*, 1, 79–92.

Office for Criminal Justice Reform (OCJR) (2005) *Policy Statement on 'A Single Inspectorate for Criminal Justice'*. London: Home Office.

Office for Public Service Reform (2003) *Inspecting for Improvement: Developing a Customer Focused Approach*. London: Cabinet Office.

Power, M. (1997) *The Audit Society: The Rituals of Verification*. Oxford: Oxford University Press.

Raine, J. W., Dunstan, E. and Patrick, R. (2006) *Enhancing Accountability in Local Policing*. London: Association of Police Authorities.

Raine, .J W. and Willson, M. J. (1993) *Managing Criminal Justice*. Hemel Hempstead: Harvester Wheatsheaf.

Tumim, S. (1992) 'The inspector as critic: The job of HM Chief Inspector of Prisons.' *The Political Quarterly 63*, 1, 5–11.

CHAPTER 7

Holistic Public Services Inspection

Steve Bundred and Clive Grace

Introduction

Public services regulation (PSR) takes many forms, and serves many different purposes. It occasionally generates confusion about what it is, who it is for, or whether it is worthwhile. Nearly 70 years ago it was derided by American critics as an unaccountable 'headless fourth branch of government' (President's Committee on Administrative Management 1937, p.32, cited by Hood *et al.* 1999, p.115). Today it is similarly derided as a burden on those who manage public services and a barrier to innovation. After decades of legislating for the growth of PSR, politicians are now signalling the retreat. In so doing, some even come close to apologising for their past misdeeds. But we will argue that developments in PSR in the UK have been rational, and that PSR has served, and continues to serve, a useful purpose. It forms part of a holistic framework for improving public services and holding to account those who spend taxpayers' money.

This chapter considers the emergence of a more holistic approach to PSR. It describes and categorises the dimensions of holistic PSR and examines its likely underlying causes and implications. We argue that the holistic theme is found:

- in the articulation of principles and ideas which apply across the field of PSR, and which are no longer confined to particular inspectorates or service sectors

- in recent moves to encourage the joining up of inspectorates both operationally and institutionally.

We suggest that holistic PSR is closely bound up with a more 'corporate' approach and the mobilisation of government at all levels to reconstruct public services for the twenty-first century under the banner of 'modernisation' and of public services reform. Within this broader context PSR is increasingly connected with other forms of accountability, performance management, and stimulants to improvement, and with the overall policy framework of public services reform. Not least among those has been the effort of the Local Government Association and the leadership that has been shown by its Improvement Board, which has helped to move thinking on significantly. The development and success of robust arrangements for peer challenge and sector-led improvement have begun to give both regulators and the government comfort in being able to place some reliance upon them. They form a part of the holistic framework and the 'corporate' approach to improvement that we describe here.

Our definition of external regulation of public services is a broad one. It embraces all facets of quality regulation, by which we mean activities aimed at improving services, reporting on their performance, and providing assurance that minimum standards are being met. It also includes a wide range of other activities that might be described as 'economic or market regulation' (see Hood *et al.* 1999). These are focused on promoting competition and protecting consumers against monopoly power. Public audit too is a form of PSR, as it is distinctive from private sector audit in the independent appointment of auditors, the wider scope of the audit and the ability of auditors to report in public. But despite the diverse manifestations of PSR, or perhaps because of them, we believe that it stands to both contribute to and be assessed as an integral part of the system for creating excellent, efficient and relevant public services which optimise public value, and at the same time to be considered as part of the accountability framework that makes taxation and public expenditure legitimate, a framework which starts with elections but – which all modern states have found – cannot end there.

Holistic PSR

There is a modern idiom of PSR which is clearly expressed in the principles which should guide it (OPSR 2002). These principles mark a departure from the approach taken during the first term of the Blair government and reflect some lessons learned from the limitations of the top-down, target-driven approach to public service improvement adopted after Blair's premiership began in 1997. The origins of the new approach can be found in the appointment of the Byatt and Lyons review (2001). Byatt and Lyons recommended that in local government the inspection of corporate capacity to deliver should provide a baseline assessment for a new, more risk-based and proportionate inspection regime. They also emphasised the need for better co-ordination and information sharing between different inspectorates. When the Office of Public Services Reform (OPSR) report *Inspecting for Improvement* (2003a) was published, the principles it articulated had already become common currency. They define the policy framework, and are now common across a range of PSR bodies in both England and the devolved administrations. According to OPSR inspection should:

- be, and be seen to be, independent
- report in public
- have wide scope, covering money, conduct, and services' performance
- reflect a user perspective
- help public bodies improve
- be risk based
- demonstrate value for money by the audit and inspection regimes themselves
- work collaboratively with other inspectors and external review agencies
- share learning
- be objective, skilled, and transparent.

These principles were articulated for the public sector, but more recently government policy has moved smartly in the direction of a common public/private approach. In his March 2005 Budget Statement the Chancellor focused heavily on regulation issues. The Hampton review (2005) which underpinned the announcement was applied also to the public sector, and both private and public sector regulation then came under the same institutional arrangements within government.

In 2006 the Audit Commission advanced a bold schema for the design of PSR which builds on the OPSR principles and engages with the (then) Chancellor's approach. It makes a distinction between first and second order principles (2006a). The former are primarily for government to address, and are described as follows:

1. The approach to the regulation of public services must sit easily within a reasonably stable, coherent framework describing how these services are to be funded, commissioned and delivered (including the role that private and voluntary sector providers are to play in the provision of services). This framework is for government to determine.

2. Within this framework, government must be clear about the role it wishes to play itself, and hence the regulatory functions that are to be reserved to government. The role of other regulators must be shaped around that.

3. It is likewise the responsibility of government to determine the overall size and shape of regulatory activity, including the number of regulatory bodies, their functions and the limits to the resources they may consume. The design of any particular regulatory regime must be consistent with this overall policy framework.

4. Changes to the framework of regulation should be infrequent, transparent and clearly explained, as should any necessary departures from core principles.

5. Regulation itself should be independent of government.

Since 2003 government has been paying particular attention to principles (1) and (3) above, manifested by a radical programme for the reform of public services and by a review of regulation. Within government the work to take forward these recommendations is now led by the Better Regulation Commission and Executive, and for both the public and private sectors the process has been conducted under the direction of a Cabinet Sub-Committee. The outcomes have been expressed most clearly in Bills that have already been presented to parliament to create new regulatory bodies for education and services to young people, although the proposals for criminal justice foundered on resistance in the House of Lords. Such measures provide a platform for regulators, in consultation with government and others, to address what the commission describes as the second order principles for the design of public sector regulation:

6. Public sector regulation must be designed so as to enable it to support government in remedying any deficiency in the model of accountability appropriate to the sector in question, whether this be a centralised model, as in the NHS, or one placing greater reliance on local democracy or a market.

7. Public sector regulation must be flexible enough to enable the right balance to be struck, at different times and in different sectors, between providing assurance to services users and taxpayers, promoting better accountability to service users, taxpayers and government; driving improvement in service performance; and enhancing value for money.

8. The specific approach to regulation in each sector must reflect the views of public service users, through the focus and outputs of its assessments, and should meet the needs of both service users and taxpayers through the incentives inherent in the funding and design of regulatory regimes.

9. Where market mechanisms exist, regulation should distinguish between commissioning and provider functions and between public and non-public providers, but should not result in market distortion by imposing undue burdens on one type of provider.

10. Regulators must themselves be accountable and must provide value for money. Regulation must be proportionate and cost-effective.

These principles reflect the importance for PSR to be part of the overall (holistic) system for ensuring accountability and driving improvement.

Joined up inspection and inspectorates

The report of Philip Hampton's (2005) review of regulation proposed that in the private sector 31 regulatory bodies were to be merged into seven, and in the public sector 11 existing inspectorates were to be merged into four, and that the cost of inspection was to be radically reduced by half. These announcements (save for criminal justice) are now being given effect. The government is cutting back and joining up and the inspectorates have been reducing significantly their inspection work. In 2001–02 the principal local government inspectorates were between them conducting 897 service inspections in the larger local authorities, of which the Audit Commission was responsible for 639. By 2005–06 the total was 214 (Audit Commission – 72). So the commission has reduced the number of inspections by 89 per cent over the last five years and the other inspectorates by nearly 50 per cent. The perception of the overall burden of the performance regime taken as a whole may not have abated significantly – which is why parallel initiatives are now under way such as the taskforce to reduce targets being chaired by Michael Frater – but the inspection burden per se has reduced a great deal.

Part of the basis for this approach is less a change of mind about the efficacy of inspection than a reflection of the progress which has been made in local authority effectiveness as evidenced in the scores of the commission's Comprehensive Performance Assessment (CPA) of local authorities and performance indicators (Communities and Local Government 2006: paras 6.8–6.11). The need for inspection of public services, it is argued, is no longer as great as it was in the early years of the Blair administration, when there was more widespread and legitimate cause for concern about the performance of many public bodies. Since then performance has improved and inspection has played an important role in securing that improvement. For reasons that are well documented in evaluations of the impact of inspection regimes, inspection does have a generally positive impact (Downe and Martin 2006, pp.466–467; Mathews and Sammons 2004, pp.475, 478). This has been reinforced by other work, including MORI's *Frontiers of Performance in Local Government IV* (Ipsos MORI 2007), which shows that not only does CPA correlate well with resident perception, but that it rewards authorities which outperform their peers serving similar populations and tends to identify underperformers in terms of resident satisfaction.

In particular there are virtually no very poorly performing local authorities and there has been general improvement in the performance of NHS services. It is of course possible that improved CPA scores may reflect authorities' increasing ability to demonstrate the kinds of characteristics and managerial practices that inspectors have been looking for rather than necessarily reflecting improvements in service outcomes or in user satisfaction. This highlights the need for such performance frameworks to be frequently challenged and tested to ensure that they are indeed measuring the right things. But the evidence that inspection does have a positive impact is strong, although local government officers argued that the overall benefits are outweighed by the burden which it imposes (Martin and Bovaird 2005). Their view that there is indeed benefit is therefore one which can be given credence, along with the quantifiable evidence available through CPA scores and performance indicators.

Alongside a more risk-based approach to inspection there has been a drive to join up the work of different inspectorates to a far greater extent. This goes beyond cutting back inspections and also reflects an appreciation of the changed character of the problems which local and other public authorities have to deal with, and the interests of public services customers, which are not just about the performance of individual services. Increasingly, the need is to form a view about the experiences that residents in each locality have with the provision of public services as a whole. Development of a more consistent approach to the assessment of the overall performance of all public bodies at the local level is therefore likely to be required, together with a more consistent approach to assessment by the different inspectorates that operate at the local level.

There have been two strands to the work involved in bringing this about. The first has been evident in joint inspections conducted by two or more statutory bodies, each with their own powers and responsibilities. An early example was the joint reviews of social services departments conducted by the Audit Commission and the Social Services Inspectorate. Other examples in the local government arena include the inspection of Youth Offending Teams. Perhaps the best and most all-embracing example of a joint inspection regime to date is the Joint Area Reviews (JARs) of children's services. These are led by Ofsted but involve a total of ten different inspectorates. They were introduced in 2005 and are conducted alongside and feed into the assessments that form part of the Audit Commission's CPA. The creation of JARs marked a recognition by government that users of public services are oblivious to the boundaries that exist between service providers, and so PSR must be equally holistic. This territorially holistic approach will be radically extended as a result of the Local Government White Paper (CLG 2006) and the Local Government and Public Involvement in Health Bill 2006 – Comprehensive Area Assessment will supersede both CPA and JARs (Audit Commission 2006b).

But bringing together so many different inspectorates within a single inspection regime also served to expose the differences and inconsistencies between them. So a separate strand of work in joining up the approach to PSR has been around reconciling, and where possible removing, differences in inspection methodologies and other elements of the inspection regimes. The system by which the results of inspection are reported is being steadily standardised, and likewise the self-assessments that inspectorates ask of inspected bodies. There is now a single timetable, available on the web, which details all the planned inspection events of the major inspectorates and seeks to avoid the possibility of inspection overload at public bodies as different inspectorates all descend at the same time. Under the White Paper proposals this joining up will strengthen further as the Audit Commission is given an extended role as the gatekeeper for all inspection affecting local authorities (CLG 2006).

Greater consistency is also being sought in other aspects of the inspection process, including the frequency with which programmed inspections take place and the use of random or short notice inspections. There are legitimate reasons why inspection methodologies may differ, but these should derive from the nature of the service being inspected rather than from differences of opinion among inspectorates about what approach is most effective. Inspecting prisons and other establishments in which vulnerable people are at risk, such as care homes, is not the same as inspecting highways maintenance. But there is an increasingly shared view across inspectorates of the need for a more joined up approach.

The Audit Commission is also undertaking work, in collaboration with other regulators, which should allow members of the public to develop a clearer understanding of the overall performance of all public service providers within their locality. A key element is the development of area profiles which provide a wide-ranging picture of the quality of life and public services in a local area by bringing together data, information and assessments for every local authority area in England. Again this activity will be strongly enhanced as a result of the

White Paper's injunction that inspection and audit should have a greater focus on citizen experience and perspectives (CLG 2006).

Part of the prize of holistic inspection is to design a regulatory regime which excludes a large number of authorities from its more onerous provisions, while still ensuring that any significant deterioration in the performance of the best councils is identified and addressed, and in a comprehensive way. Such a regime could draw on, and suitably adapt, the proposal put forward by Byatt and Lyons:

> Following the Base Line inspection, the authority would review both its plans and its capacity to achieve them. This would be expected to lead to a programme of organisational development, capacity building and specific proposals for the improvement of individual services. ...During each subsequent year of the cycle...the focus would shift radically towards progress made against performance improvement plans, drawing on evidence from performance indicators...and other developmental activities. Local auditors would contribute from their own knowledge of the organisation. (Byatt and Lyons 2001, para 44 *et seq.*)

This aspiration has come a lot closer through the provisions of the 2006 English Local Government White Paper for a joined up 'annual risk assessment' of each local authority area, addressed to the Local Strategic Partnership, between the relevant public service inspectorates, led by the Audit Commision (CLG 2006). This will be the basis for triggering inspection where it is needed, coupled with annual judgements on an authority's 'direction of travel' and its use of resources, both scored on a basis of comparability between authorities.

A holistic approach also requires that PSR is closer to the problem. In the traditional idiom PSR made its assessment after the event – it followed on behind, explaining what had gone wrong or giving assurance that things had been done broadly right. To improve its effectiveness as a force in improvement, especially in a rapidly changing world of public services, PSR needs to work alongside the services reviewed, providing feedback almost in 'real time', linked where possible to more rigorous self-assessment by inspected bodies themselves.

In relation to local government, the CPA in England, the Wales Programme for Improvement, and Best Value Audits in Scotland are all 'holistic' insofar as they look at the whole organisation and assess both the corporate and service aspects, including vertical aspects (Grace 2007). They have transcended the individual service-based methods of early Best Value approaches. But there have been other developments in method which are also holistic. What they have in common is that the method being used is tailored to risks and issues as they are experienced in the real world by public service bodies and by service users and the public. They aim to overcome the dangers of silo approaches and include the following:

- Looking at the experience of the user/customer either in relation to a particular service or, for example, by looking at the 'patient pathway' along which a patient travels if she or he has a particular condition.

- Looking at a local community or a local area and assessing how public services are serving that community as a whole, including the way in which those services are working together in partnership for the benefit of a locality.

- Making an assessment of the effectiveness or impact of a particular policy from its creation through the various delivery bodies which may be responsible for giving effect to it on the ground, and through to the users'/customers' experience ('delivery chain' or 'policy-to-delivery' review).

- Taking a 'whole systems' approach when looking at, for example, health and social care, in which social care, primary care and secondary care form part of one whole system, and where the individual elements cannot sensibly be assessed in isolation.

- Having regard to the need to provide a value for money perspective of government policies and programmes concerned with 'big picture' issues such as sustainable development, long-term public health issues such as obesity (the topic of a recent Audit Commission/National Audit Office (NAO) joint study) , and fundamental questions facing society such as climate change.

- Combining a customer and a territorial perspective as in the concept of Comprehensive Area Assessments.

At an operational level, the NAO and Audit Commission have collaborated in the assessment of the Efficiency Technical Notes prepared by government departments to demonstrate implementation of the Gershon efficiency recommendations. They have also collaborated on 'delivery chain analysis' of some key PSA targets, which can only be successfully achieved if the delivery chain stretching from government and through local delivery bodies to customers and users is properly connected and co-ordinated.

Finally under this heading of the holistic joining up of inspection and inspectorates it is important to note that institutional consolidation in England has developed in parallel with what looks at first blush like a counter-trend in the creation of the Wales Audit Office from the relevant parts of the Audit Commission and the NAO, broadly echoing the Scottish arrangements. At the same time there are recent moves in Wales (and some stirrings in Scotland also) to achieve the complete consolidation of all the major public service inspectorates in the Wales Audit Office, which would amount to a joining up on a grand scale within Wales, and might set a tone for the UK as a whole.

A corporate approach

Along with other forms of regulation, the growth of inspection under this government did not come about by accident. It has been fundamental to the Blair government's approach. But it was not the Blair government that started the process, which began with the privatisation of state monopolies in the Thatcher years. Between 1979 and 1997 the government generated £68.8 billion from well over 100 separate acts of privatisation and sale of assets. In many instances the privatisation was accompanied by the creation of a new regulator to ensure decent service quality and prevent abuse of monopoly power – Ofwat, Ofcom, Ofgem, and so on.

The growth of public sector inspection in the first two terms of the Blair government was prompted by other equally good reasons. The government was committed to substantial increases in spending on public services and was pledged to improve their performance. Modernising public services was central to successive election manifestos. That was what the government had promised to do. Reducing hospital waiting lists and improving school standards were to be the key tests of the government's success or failure. But ministers were anxious to ensure that the improvements in the quality of public services took place. They needed to be able to demonstrate that the promises were being fulfilled. So the quid pro quo for extra cash was centrally imposed targets and tight performance management. This was reinforced by increased inspection as one means by which the government could both stimulate and support reform and also demonstrate that it was working.

The growth of inspection was a price in additional accountability to be paid by managers of public services in return for the extra money they received. It helped to make the trebling of expenditure on the NHS and the 39 per cent real increase in grants to local authorities politically acceptable, and was part of how government gave practical effect to the mantra of 'investment *and* reform'. This approach echoed the underlying principles of the regulation of private sector monopolies, and helps to explain why post-Hampton private and public sector regulation was jointly brigaded under the Better Regulation Executive/Commission. It recognised that most public services are provided in conditions of monopoly supply, with the regulation of monopolies being a proper and indeed a normal function of government. There might be many different providers in the market, as in the cases of waste collection or leisure management, for example, but for the most part, public services customers can only get the provider that a particular council chooses to contract with, and the service that is specified in the contract. For those who rely on monopoly public

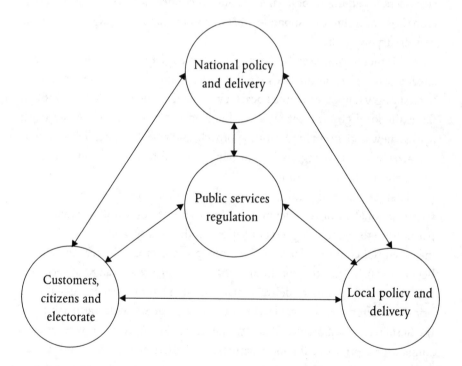

FIGURE 7.1 RELATIONSHIP BETWEEN PUBLIC SERVICES REGULATION, NATIONAL POLICY AND DELIVERY, LOCAL POLICY AND DELIVERY AND CUSTOMERS, CITIZENS AND ELECTORATE

services to deliver *for* them or *to* them, regulation provides assurance and can also be a way to stimulate improvement, as is standard governmental practice for private sector monopolies.

The closeness of the relationship between government policy in relation to public services and its reform, the needs of customers to have monopolies properly regulated, and the developing role of PSR (its 'modern idiom' or 'emerging new paradigm', as it has been termed by Grace 2003, 2005) can be best understood in terms of the holistic relationships which are being developed between the policymakers who decide what services should be provided, the bodies actually providing services and the customers who use them. The approach can best be depicted as shown in Figure 7.1.

PSR bodies have relationships with the audited bodies, with policymakers and with citizens and customers. Moreover, each of these connections is two-way. Thus, policymakers try to get feedback from delivery agents to help them develop policy more adroitly. Delivery agents also listen much more to customers. In addition, policymakers aim to connect directly to customers in terms both of trying to respond to what they want and informing them of what they are trying to do.

This picture was used by Grace (2005) in depicting the changes that had already taken place in the UK's public service audit and inspection, but it has been strongly reinforced by the Local Government White Paper (CLG 2006). As far as the local government sector in England is concerned, the White Paper marks a new high point in a holistic approach, and reveals the explicit corporate character which is being applied to public service reform and improvement. There are several aspects to this.

First, central and local government are to share key priorities – a single set of national priority outcomes for local authorities working alone or in partnership to create a single set of national indicators against which all will be measured (CLG 2006). These will be incorporated in Local Area Agreements between central government, local authorities, and a wide range of local and national partners, as the 'delivery plan' for these priorities, along with the priorities determined at local level through the Local Strategic Partnership and the Sustainable Community Strategy. The Local Area Agreement will set out a single set of priorities for local partners, and there will be a duty for local authorities and other local partners to work together to agree their priorities. The partners who will be placed under this duty include police, probation, youth offending teams, primary care trusts, health trusts, learning and skills councils, the Health and Safety Executive, the Environment Agency, the Highways Agency, Regional Development Agencies and joint waste disposal authorities, among others.

Second, citizens and users are to be placed at the heart of service commissioning, and the new performance framework is to be designed to support citizen involvement and secure better outcomes (CLG 2006). The government will encourage local authorities to have more systematic intelligence on local people's needs and views, and they will explore with local authorities how to improve information management, including streamlining national reporting systems, ensuring data quality and supporting the development of local information systems (CLG 2006). Both of these express a strengthening of the relationships described in Figure 7.1 between government, local government and citizens. These are addressed directly when the White Paper says that strong, effective local organisations and local partnerships will be needed to deliver the outcomes that national government and local people want to see (CLG 2006).

The third aspect is the explicit way in which the inspectorates – principally the Audit Commission in this case – are to underpin these strengthening three-way relationships. Under the new performance framework to be implemented by 2009, local authorities will report annually on performance against the targets in the LAA including reporting on improvement targets agreed against national priorities to central government and also as a basis of reporting to local people on progress. This should reflect a robust self-assessment of progress due in the year and risks for future delivery. Meanwhile, the Audit Commission is charged with ensuring that audit and inspection have a greater focus on citizen experience and perspectives, and that the results of audit, assessment and inspection become more publicly accessible (CLG 2006).

Within the performance framework, the need for inspection will depend primarily on the basis of the risk judgements. The relevant public services inspectorates will each have a statutory duty to co-operate with each other and to manage the burden of inspection on individual organisations within their sector. The Audit Commission will be the gatekeeper for all inspections affecting local authorities (CLG 2006). So the tightening co-operation and co-ordination among partners at local level is to be mirrored by a parallel tightening among the inspectorates. Further, the commission is tasked with ensuring that the local government information management systems that provide the necessary citizen information and intelligence are themselves up to scratch.

All of this adds up in our view to a significantly stronger corporate approach by government, and a much stronger conscious orchestration of national priorities, local delivery and citizen needs, coupled with the explicit use of inspectorates to inform and enforce the alignment between them. Even where diversity is encouraged – for example, in the promotion of greater citizen choice and in greater diversity of supply through 'holistic commissioning' – that also is to be enforced through the more corporate framework, including if necessary strengthening the auditor's ability to respond to complaints from service providers about unfair and unlawful procurement (CLG 2006).

The White Paper is, of course, an English affair. But while there are differences which derive from UK devolution, PSR can still occupy a similar space in the process of public services reform and improvement in each specific jurisdiction. Wales, for example, has explicitly chosen not to use the market or competition, external judgements and categorisations, 'naming and shaming', excessive targets, and league tables, and so on. The Welsh Assembly Government has preferred the approach that has been spelt out in some detail in *Making the Connections* (WAG 2004), and has also been subject to review by an inquiry team led by Sir Jeremy Beecham (WAG 2006). However, the new relationships described above for PSR remain relevant in Wales as in England, albeit that the content of those relationships differs.

As part of this more integrated set of relationships with policymakers, delivery bodies, and customers, it is easier to see that all PSR activity forms a part of what may be seen in portmanteau terms as the emerging 'fourth arm of governance'. This fourth arm directly provides or facilitates scrutiny of government. It also provides a review function to help drive improvement. It is the 'headless fourth branch of government' identified by Roosevelt's 1937 Committee.

This 'fourth branch' is not confined to PSR bodies. Modern states have developed a whole range of mechanisms through which government is held to account and its actions scrutinised, both in relation to individual decisions and claims for redress and at the wider policy level. These mechanisms operate within each of the three principal branches of government – legislative, judicial and executive – as well as directly to the Crown. So within the legislative arm of governance in the UK there is the system of select and scrutiny committees, such as in parliament itself, and through the Audit Committee and the Subject Committees of the National Assembly for Wales. In the judicial arm, the special judicial subsystem of public law has developed to provide redress through judicial review and many mechanisms of appeal and challenge. The executive branch itself has created explicit mechanisms to provide a source of review and scrutiny – such as the Audit Commission, for example, which is a public corporation sponsored by the Department for Communities and Local Government and the Department of Health. So there are two senses here in which the 'holistic' theme is given effect – both through the more holistic approach which links national policy, local delivery, and customers, all with PSR bodies, but also between the various PSR bodies.

Risks and opportunities

This chapter has charted the rise of the 'holistic' approach to PSR and has argued that this is a welcome development which has considerable potential to further enhance the effectiveness of public services regulation. As service providers get better and more confident, as central government continues to improve its capacity to steer public services reform, and as regulators understand their new role better, there opens up the prospect of more mature relationships in which the connections between national, local and citizen levels are explicit; the role of PSR bodies is acknowledged; independence continues to be respected and protected; PSR is optimal rather than minimal; and where PSR is accepted and even welcomed by the regulated. Such an approach would also strengthen a trend towards the 'co-production' of accountability and of service improvement, principally through a much stronger emphasis on self-regulation and self-improvement, and 'residual' inspection based on continually declining risk, coupled with an enhanced 'co-production' role for citizens and customers. In our view that would be a desirable state of affairs, which should be encouraged and if possible speeded up.

This is an optimistic picture, and some will no doubt see it as too rosy by half, and we emphasise that it will not be achieved without strenuous effort to continue to reduce the burden of accountability as well as to maximise its benefit. But in our view such an approach is not only attainable but essential, in the interests of local government and its partners as well as customers and citizens. This is illustrated in our view by another aspect of the 2006 Local

Government White Paper when it argues at length for the involvement of local government and its partners in tackling some of the most trenchant national and even global challenges facing the UK and its people and communities – issues of climate change, economic development, and health, for example. These are issues that can neither be tackled locally or nationally in isolation, but only in concert between levels of government which are confident and effective in their own spheres, and are fit for purpose in responding to the needs of the citizens and customers of public services and in working together on the longer-term challenges. The role of modern PSR should be both to help hold government at all levels to account in performing these difficult tasks, and also to help them improve their capacities and capabilities in doing so. A more holistic, corporate approach in public services delivery and reform, and in the PSR which performs those roles, holds as good a prospect as any of achieving them.

References

Audit Commission (2006a) *The Future of Regulation.* London: Audit Commission.

Audit Commission (2006b) *Assessment of Local Services Beyond 2008.* London: Audit Commission.

Byatt, I. and Lyons, M. (2001) *The Role of External Review in Improving Performance.* London: HM Treasury.

Communities and Local Government (CLG) (2006) *Strong and Prosperous Communities: The Local Government White Paper.* London: Communities and Local Government.

Downe, J. and Martin, S. J. (2006) 'Joined up policy in practice? The coherence and impacts of the local government modernisation agenda.' *Local Government Studies 32,* 4, 465–488.

Grace, C. (2003) 'Regulation: The modern idiom.' *Public Money and Management 23,* 2, 73–75.

Grace, C. (2005) 'Change and Improvement in Audit and Inspection: A Strategic approach for the 21st century.' *Local Government Studies 31,* 5, 575–596.

Grace, C. (ed.) (2007) *Comparing for Improvement.* London: Solace Foundation Imprint.

Hampton, P. (2005) *Reducing Administrative Burdens: Effective Inspection and Enforcement.* London: HM Treasury.

Hood, C., Scott, C., James, O., Jones, G. and Travers, T. (1999) *Regulation Inside Government.* Oxford: Oxford University Press.

Ipsos MORI (2007) *Frontiers of Performance in Local Government IV.* London: Ipsos MORI.

Martin, S. J. and Bovaird, A. G. (2005) *Progress Report on Service Improvement in Local Government.* London: Office of the Deputy Prime Minister.

Mathews, P. and Sammons, P. (2004) *Improvement through Inspection.* London: HMI 2244 Ofsted.

Office of Public Services Reform (OPSR) (2002) *Principles of Public Services Reform.* London: Cabinet Office.

Office of Public Services Reform (2003) *Inspecting for Improvement.* London: Cabinet Office.

Welsh Assembly Government (WAG) (2004) *Making the Connections: Delivering Better Services for Wales.* Cardiff: Welsh Assembly Government.

Welsh Assembly Government (WAG) (2006) *Making the Connections: Beyond Boundaries.* Cardiff: Welsh Assembly Government.

Bibliograpy

Audit Commission (2005) *CPA: The Harder Test.* London: Audit Commission.

Audit Commission (2008) *The Evolution of Regulation.* London: Audit Commission.

Black, B. (2004) *Holding to Account and Helping to Improve.* Edinburgh: Audit Scotland.

Black, B. (2006) *Public Service Improvement. The Conditions for Success and the Scottish Experience.* Edinburgh: Audit Scotland.

Bundred, S. (2005) 'Regulating Reformed Public Services.' In M. Bichard and C. Grace (eds) *Perspectives on the Third Term: The Way Ahead.* London: Solace Foundation Imprint.

Davis, H., Downe, J. and Martin, S. J. (2004) *The Changing Role of Audit Commission Inspection of Local Government.* London: Audit Commission.

Grace, C., Downe, J., Martin, S. J. and Nutley, S. M. (2007) *Decisive Moment: The Independent Review of the Best Value Audit Process.* Edinburgh: Audit Scotland.

Hood, C., James, O. and Scott, C. (2000) 'Regulation of government: Has it increased, is it increasing, should it be diminished?' *Public Administration 78,* 2, 283–304.

Martin, S. J. (2002) 'The modernisation of UK local government: Markets, managers, monitors and mixed fortunes.' *Public Management Review 4,* 3, 291–307.

Martin, S. J. (2005) 'Public Service improvement: Current developments and future research agendas.' *Local Government Studies 31,* 2, 531–540.

Office of Public Services Reform (2003) *The Government's Policy on Inspection of Public Services.* London: Cabinet Office.

Power, M. (1994) *The Audit Explosion.* London: Demos.

Power, M. (2003) 'Evaluating the audit explosion.' *Law and Policy 25,* 3, 185–202.

Rhodes, R. A. W. (1994) 'The hollowing out of the state: The changing nature of the public service in britain.' *Political Quarterly 65,* 2, 138–151.

Wales Audit Office (WAO) (2006) *Wales Programme for Improvement Annual Report 2004/5.* Cardiff: Welsh Audit Office.

Welsh Assembly Government (WAG) (2005) *Regulation and Inspection of Public Services in Wales, National Assembly for Wales Local Government and Public Services Committee.* Cardiff: Welsh Assembly Government.

CHAPTER 8

Performance Paradoxes
The Politics of Evaluation in Public Services

John Clarke

Introduction

The expansion of systems for scrutinising and evaluating the performance of public services has received much academic attention (e.g. Davis, Downe and Martin 2001; Hood *et al.* 1998; Humphrey 2002; Paton 2003; Pollitt *et al.* 1999; Power 1997). In this chapter, I intend to explore some of the paradoxes and forms of politics associated with the development of these systems. I draw out the international and national politics of inspection in relation to the themes of transparency and good governance before examining the 'paradox of government' in relation to public services. I then consider the 'paradox of independence' embedded in the institutional organisation of evaluation and the 'paradox of publicness' as a focus of competing representations of the public interest. Finally, I turn to the 'paradox of success' that is associated with the practice of evaluation and its outcomes. Each of these paradoxes is associated with different forms and modes of politics – as agents, groups and organisations strive to claim 'success' in representing the public interest. I use 'evaluation' to refer to the array of agencies that audit, inspect and scrutinise the provision of public services.

This is a slightly different view of scrutiny and evaluation from that offered in official accounts that stress the themes of transparency, accountability, good governance and continuous improvement (on the part of services and their evaluators). This paradox-centred account is not a story about the distortion of the pure principles of inspection, audit, or evaluation. This is not a process in which 'politics' enters to undermine or corrupt innocent intentions or practices. On the contrary, these paradoxes – and the possibilities for politics that they create – are built into the intentions, design and implementation of performance evaluation in public services.

Public service performance
The paradox of government

The expansion of public service performance evaluation in its many forms is associated with two interrelated processes: the reconstruction of the organisational forms of states (variously branded as the 'new Public Management' and 'reinventing government', Hood 1991; Osborne and Gaebler 1992; see also Clarke and Newman 1997) and the development of what Larner and Walters (2004) call 'global governmentalities': ways of thinking about the regulation of economic, social and political action that work across national boundaries. These globalising conceptions include notions of accountability, transparency and good governance that circulate through international organisations such as the World Bank and International Monetary Fund (see Harper 2000; West and Sanders 2003). These organisations provide 'templates and benchmarks' against which national governments can place (and, of course, evaluate) their own public service and public management reform programmes.

In a complex interaction with these globalising dynamics, national state systems have been subjected to extensive organisational remodelling and refurbishment. I want to highlight a number of distinctive features here that create the institutional landscape in which the expansion of performance evaluation 'makes sense'. They form the contexts in which systems of evaluation appear reasonable, plausible and necessary. This is a brief list but I hope it makes clear the multiple dynamics that have been in play in programmes of state reform.

First is the *fiscalization of discourses* about public services, welfare provision and other state-centred activities (Prince 2001). This refers to the ways in which public and political debate about policies, governmental objectives and forms of organising to achieve them have been increasingly placed within 'fiscal' frames: about acceptable levels of taxation and public spending; about the relationship between public spending and national competitiveness; about the 'efficiency' of provision (and calculations of its 'value for money'). Stein describes the widespread use (and slippery meanings) of 'efficiency' as a cult:

> The cult of efficiency, like other cults, advances political purposes and agendas. In our post-industrial age, efficiency is often a code word for an attack on the sclerotic, unresponsive, and anachronistic state, the detritus of the industrial age that fits poorly with our times. The state is branded as wasteful, and market mechanisms are heralded as the efficient alternative. (Stein 2001, p.7)

Second, Stein's comments point to the construction of *new types of organisational forms* for the production, distribution and management of public services (Clarke 2006). These include 'outsourcing' to preferred market suppliers; the greater engagement of voluntary sector organisation; the creation of 'hybrid' organisations that work across the increasingly blurred boundary between public and private sectors; and finally the increasing 'devolution of responsibility' to individuals, families and households to provide for their own well-being. But all of these different organisational forms are expected to behave in 'businesslike' ways and to be 'well managed'. Such norms – it is claimed – will drive improvements in efficiency and quality (Cutler and Waine 1997). The effect is to create a more dispersed and complex field of 'public services' (sometimes described as 'fragmentation') that poses problems of co-ordination and control for governments.

Third, these changes have taken place in the context of changing relationships between governments and the governed. In western societies, at least, these relationships seem marked by several intersecting tendencies: disaffection from processes of official politics (lower involvement in activities ranging from membership of parties through to voting); increasing scepticism or cynicism about politics and politicians; and increasing mobilisations outside of conventional politics around different sorts of interests and identities (from environmentalism through to 'countryside' and 'fathers' movements in the UK). These different tendencies have paradoxical consequences for governments and the role of the state in contemporary societies. Hansen and Stepputat pick up a version of this paradox (what they call the 'paradox of inadequacy and indispensability') when they argue:

> The paradox seems to be that while the authority of the state in constantly questioned and functionally undermined, there are growing pressures on states to confer full-fledged rights and entitlements on ever more citizens, to confer recognition and visibility on ever more institutions, movements or organizations, and a growing demand on states from the

so-called international community to address development problems effectively and to promote a 'human rights culture'. (Hansen and Stepputat
2001, p.2)

This paradox is intensified in the case of public services. Governments persistently promise to reform, improve or modernise public services, not least
because publics continue to want publicly provided services to support them in
the face of both old and new 'risks'. Meanwhile, governments have adopted a
position of mistrust in relation to public service providers. The logic of market
superiority (as against sclerotic and anachronistic state bureaucracies) means
that public services should be subjected to the improving discipline of market
dynamics. Where such dynamics cannot be achieved by direct 'outsourcing',
governments have tried to find the mechanisms through which to mimic market
dynamics, creating internal or quasi-market forms; creating 'competition
regimes' between organisations; and creating 'virtual consumers' (Clarke 2006;
Miller 2005). The idea of responding to 'consumer expectations' and providing
reliable information have played a central role in UK public service reform:

> The challenges and demands on today's public services are very different
> from those of the post-war years. The rationing culture which survived
> after the war, in treating everyone the same, often overlooked individuals'
> different needs and aspirations. Rising standards, a more diverse society
> and a steadily stronger consumer culture have increased the demand for
> good quality schools, hospitals and other public services, and at the same
> time brought expectations of greater choice, responsiveness, accessibility
> and flexibility. (Office of Public Services Reform 2002, p.8)

It is worth noting one more twist in the paradox. As governments strive to
reform public services and produce 'improvements', they encounter an increasingly sceptical public unwilling to believe things that they are told by
politicians. Evaluation systems and agencies promise a way out of this paradox
of government: independent and expert agencies that can assess performance
and its improvement 'at arm's length' from government. This leads unerringly
to the second paradox: the paradox of independence.

Reliable sources?

The paradox of independence

Independence is a critical dimension of the rise of performance evaluation systems. Transparency and accountability need to be guaranteed by agents and agencies who can be 'trusted' to provide accurate and reliable information that is untainted by affinities and attachments (this is discussed at greater length in Clarke 2005a). There are several ways in which independence can be claimed and legitimated, all of which are in circulation in the way that evaluation agencies represent themselves. Here I explore four dimensions of independence: the technical, institutional, political and social. Technical claims refer to the techniques, technologies, methods and approaches that trained experts put to work in the process of doing evaluation. Institutional claims rest on separation between the evaluation agency and other governmental bodies. Institutional independence has a double dynamic: evaluators need to be seen as independent from government and from the evaluated organisations. Political independence refers, in the world of public services, to separation from party political attachments, obligations or loyalties. Finally, the social dimension of independence involves questions of representativeness: how do those who stand in judgement 'represent' the public? Representativeness has become an increasingly contested issue in relation to public institutions, especially in terms of their sociodemographic composition. All of these bases for claiming independence are always potentially vulnerable to counterclaims and challenges.

The *technical* dimension involves challenges about the reliability and robustness of methodologies and their implementation, affecting how claims about evaluations, judgements and evidence are perceived and received. Accountancy practice – the basis for conventional audit – has been the 'master' methodology in this field but other forms of evaluation and scrutiny have been more vulnerable to challenges to their epistemology, methodology and practice. There have, for example, been persistent questions about the reliability and replicability of the methodologies employed by inspectorates, and about the relationship between evidence and evaluation. Such challenges are contested in return, through claims about the robustness of the methodological practices of evaluation or their future perfectibility. Downe and Martin offer a critical reflection on the 'technical' character of the Audit Commission's 'Best Value' inspections:

Our contention is that whilst the Audit Commission has successfully presented its work as being underpinned by a rigorous process which is applied consistently across all services, the air of quasi-scientific 'objectivity' which attaches to both the inspection methodology itself and to the reports it produces belies the often less than totally clear cut-cut basis on which judgements are made by inspectors. (Downe and Martin 2007a, p.24; see also Harper 2000 on IMF missions)

The *institutional* dimension involves challenges about the scale of the distance between scrutiny agencies and other areas of government that is needed to create and maintain independence. The UK government's 2003 policy statement on the Inspection of Public Services defines inspection as 'an external review that should be independent of the service providers' (Office of Public Services Reform 2003, p.3). To the extent that agencies are evaluating the implementation of government policy, they risk being viewed as the agents of government. The degree of perceived institutional independence is also affected by the ways in which the role of audit and evaluation agencies has expanded and shifted. In particular, the blurring of lines between evaluation and consultancy/prescription also raises issues about institutional independence (as indeed it has in corporate sector practices of accounting and audit post-Enron).

The *political* dimension of instability involves challenges that address the conflation of party, government, policy and evaluation. Challenges to the political independence of scrutiny agencies may address the too close identification between governmental policy and party interest (particularly in an adversarial polity, such as the UK). Evaluation agencies tend to make every effort to behave in politically neutral ways (briefing all parties, eschewing direct political representation, etc.). Labour governments since 1997 have made a virtue of 'evidence based policy' – and a commitment to eschew 'ideology' in favour of a pragmatic commitment that 'what counts is what works' (Davies, Nutley and Smith 2000; Trinder and Reynolds 2000). This puts evaluative agencies in a highly visible – and potentially vulnerable – place in the policy process. Since New Labour have, in practice, combined 'pragmatism' with the evangelical pursuit of selected policies (the 'one best way', such as in the pursuit of Public–Private Partnerships), evaluation and evidence are persistently at risk of 'contamination' from political zeal (Clarke 2005b).

It is always difficult to 'depoliticise' policy choices, because the realm of politics extends beyond issues of party affiliation. While scrutiny agencies and agents may be independent of parties, they may nevertheless take up identifiable positions within the politicised field of choices about policy, practice, or even organisational design. Despite efforts to claim pragmatism, evidence-based, and non-ideological foundations for policy formation, policy and practice in public services has remained 'contentious' – the focus of contending philosophical, moral, professional and political judgements (see, inter alia, Stein 2001; Strathern 2000).

Finally, the *social* dimension of independence has been relatively invisible in relation to evaluation regimes. Nevertheless, questions of social composition, identity and representation have been raised in relation to almost all forms of public service (from the judiciary to social services). It seems unlikely that evaluation agencies will remain immune to questions about who they are and what they stand for. Challenges around issues of representation and representativeness demand something other than institutional, technical or political neutrality. They claim that social composition has pertinent *organisational effects* – about what identities, interests and experiences can be taken account of in serving a complex and differentiated public. The linked question is whether social composition has *political effects* – creating and sustaining policies that reproduce divisions and inequalities. If evaluators are to take a 'user perspective' (ODPM/HM Treasury 2005, p.31; OPSR 2003), then in what ways should they be representative of service users? At present, though, the technical, institutional, professional modes of independence appear to have insulated evaluation agencies against such 'social' challenges.

These vulnerabilities are the site of political work in the larger sense. At the macro level, agencies and agents affirm independence claims, produce evidence or testimony to their autonomy, and reassert the promise of technical improvement. At the micro level, evaluators and those being evaluated construct negotiated practices of 'evaluation' – in which the management of performance and interaction is a task for both parties, but where both parties must collude in the 'production of truth and transparency' (Clarke 2005b). Independence is not a condition that can be proven or disproved. Rather it is a claim that must be continually sustained and revitalised in practice.

Dogging public services
The paradox of publicness

A favoured media image of evaluation agencies is that of the 'watchdog' but, as Robert Hackett has suggested, there are other sorts of metaphorical dogs. Hackett's own analysis deals with the relationship between the news media and questions of civic equality, but has suggestive parallels with the relationship between evaluation agencies and the public interest. He discusses a longstanding conception of the news media as watchdog:

> The standard view presents journalism as the Great Leveller – a builder of a sense of local and national community, but also a righter of wrongs, a humbler of the mighty, a watchdog against the abuse of power, and agent to 'comfort the afflicted and afflict the comfortable'. The commercial press of the 1800s, the world's first mass medium was born with a profound democratic promise: to present information without fear or favour, to make it accessible to everyone, and to foster public rationality based on equal access to relevant facts. (Hackett 2001, p.197)

Representations of evaluative agencies have many echoes of this conception of the watchdog: collecting and publicising information; making such information universally accessible and attempting to foster 'public rationality'. Such 'watchdogs' aim to protect the public against poor quality services through multiple means: naming poor performers 'without fear or favour'; spreading 'best practice' and enabling people using public services to make informed, rational choices based on comparative evidence. Hackett goes on to raise the possibility of thinking of the media as 'mad dogs':

> One avenue of critique sees journalism as having shifted from watchdog to mad dog, mindlessly attacking authority (especially governments), avoiding serious news about public affairs in favour of scandals, celebrities and 'infotainment'. In doing so, the media are reputedly blocking government's efforts to communicate with citizens and even threatening the legitimacy of democratic public authority. (Hackett 2001, p.198)

This seems less readily applicable to public service evaluation agencies, yet their reputation for 'independence' is, as I noted above, often sustained through reference to their 'challenges' to government or public service providers. There are also tensions around conflicting claims to represent the public and its interests, especially in the field of services that are provided or organised by local government. There are at least three such claims in play:

1.   National governments claim an electoral 'mandate' to represent the public interest and have increasingly come to position themselves as the 'people's champions' in relation to public service providers (Clarke 2005b).

2.   Local governments claim an electoral mandate to represent their 'local' public and its interests in their organisation and provision of public services or in local 'partnership' arrangements with other organisations and agencies.

3.   Evaluative agencies claim to provide an evidential basis for protecting and enhancing the public interest (understood as a combination of a fiduciary understanding of the taxpayers interest and a quality/standards model of the consumer interest (Clarke 2005b; Cooper 1998).

Viewed in these terms, evaluative agencies have the potential to function as Hackett's 'mad dogs', at least in the sense of disrupting governmental claims and authority. The field of claims to represent the public interest is, of course, more crowded than this in practice, containing many other organisations that claim to be the 'voice' of the public or specific segments or interests within the public (social movements, non-government organisations, government-operated NGOs, and so on). The news media also claim 'public interest' representation in their reporting on public services (whether in watchdog or mad dog mode). Hackett's third version of media doggery is as 'lap dogs':

> Another critique sees the media not as mad dogs, but as lap dogs, excessively subservient to the economic and political elite…the media are seen to legitimize the unjust policies and privileges of the state and corporations while muzzling the voices of fundamental dissent and marginalizing ordinary citizens from political debate, positioning them as passive spectators. (Hackett, 2001, p.198)

Again, the connections to evaluative agencies look more tenuous than in their 'watchdog' image. But to the extent that the agenda of evaluative agencies' investigations is framed by governmental policy, conceptions of the public interest and, increasingly, conceptions of the public as consumers of services, then evaluative agencies risk being seen as government 'lap dogs', even if they occasionally bite the hand that feeds them.

Similarly, the rationalist model of evaluation and information (combined with populist reportage techniques such as 'league tables' and 'star ratings') may diminish public debate about politics, policy and priorities, promoting instead a collusive relationship with government policy choices and a consumer/ spectator position for individuated citizens (Needham 2003). The risk of being perceived to be agents of government is increased by the tendency for independence to be blurred when agencies are expected to act as 'consultants' and 'critical friends', proposing advice and support for improvement (Day and Klein 1990). Downe and Martin refer to this as the 'transition from independent "watchdog" to helpful "guide dog"' (2007b, p.228), filling out the dog imagery still further.

My argument is not that evaluative agencies are one or other of these 'dogs', but that the contexts and complexity of their roles make it likely that they will be seen as all three (or four) by different groups at different times. Both governments and the agencies have aspired to the image of the watchdog: the impartial and independent purveyor of evidence-based judgements. There has been a growing use of agencies as 'guide dogs' driven by the performance improvement agenda (and partly in response to providers becoming tired of being savaged by 'mad dogs', or at least experiencing evaluation as expensive, burdensome, time consuming and intrusive). Such agencies constantly run the risk of being seen (especially by a hostile news media) as 'lap dogs' – in collusion with either the government or service providers.

Competitive evaluation
The paradox of success

'Success' is central to the system of public services performance evaluation. Success is both an effect of, and a dynamic in, the process of evaluation. Evaluation seeks to produce success in general (systemically), while also distinguishing between particular organisational successes and failures. The regime of evaluation in the UK has been comparative-competitive: evaluating performances against success criteria (targets, standards, benchmarks, etc.) and rating or ranking the performance of individual performance. The setting of targets, the scrutiny of organisations and the measurement of performance are both constructed and constitutive processes. Targets, criteria, methods and their implementation in the practice of evaluation are contestable, even though the process and its results are represented as 'categorical' (Paton 2003, p.29; see also Humphrey 2002). Schram and Soss (2002) have explored how the evaluative criteria for welfare reform in the US were framed and applied in practice. For example, the selection of caseload levels and numbers of programme leavers as 'outcomes' measures reflected particular views about welfare, poverty and dependency and obscured other possibilities, such as poverty reduction, (2002, p.193). They highlight the political significance of 'success':

> The discursive processes that we have highlighted…merit close attention because judgements of policy success and failure are more than just political outcomes; they are also political forces. Beliefs about which policies are known failures and which have been shown to succeed set the parameters for a 'reasonable' debate over the shape of future legislation. Reputations for developing successful ideas confer authority, giving some advocates greater access and influence in the legislative process. Public officials who are able to claim credit for policy success hold a political resource that bestows advantage in both electoral and legislative contests. (Schram and Soss 2002, p.200)

The construction of evaluation as a process of co-ordinating dispersed public service provision has created different versions of 'success' (and multiple interests in being successful). It is a process that is about the production of success (and failure): the comparative-competitive model of performance evaluation is intended to rank 'winners and losers'. This process predisposes people to attempt to be successful. Organisational analysts have long known that 'what gets measured is what gets done' by focusing organisational performance on the criteria of evaluation. These evaluation dynamics produce many actors with an interest in 'success':

- the government and specific ministers (demonstrating their capacity to 'deliver')

- service or agency heads (demonstrating their capacity to 'improve' the service)

- organisations (demonstrating their relative effectiveness)

- managers/leaders in organisations (demonstrating their ability to innovate, improve or 'turn round failing organisations').

Evaluation agencies also have an interest in success. They need to demonstrate that scrutiny 'works' – improving the performance of the service. They also need to show that earlier recommendations (of policy, practice or organisational design) have had the desired effect. Paradoxically, scrutiny agencies need to both promote success and look 'tough' by identifying 'failure', so as to resist charges of producer capture.

Finally, as Schram and Soss (2002) argue, 'success' is a political resource. It is a resource that matters to organisations, managers and political representatives, especially in competitive or marketised systems of service provision. 'Success' provides a competitive edge – in relation to resources, political access and 'consumers' (directly and indirectly). Organisations must tell 'success stories' (and suppress or invalidate non-success stories) as a condition of organisational reproduction and development. The effect is a 'success spiral' in which all participants to the process have an inflationary interest in producing 'success'. In such an inflationary context, there are potential problems about how audiences perceive and respond to success claims.

Although scrutiny agencies publish their reports, commentaries and evaluations, these seem not to have reached the 'general reader'. There remains a gap between the imagined 'active citizen-consumer' scrutinising performance evaluations and making rational/responsible choices, and the everyday practices of members of the public (Clarke et al. 2007). A survey for the Office for Public Service Reform 'revealed that the public has a generally low recognition of inspectorates' with Ofsted the most recognised, by 17 per cent of those surveyed (OPSR 2003, p.23). Evaluation reports circulate mainly in political and policy networks so that taxpayers/consumers mainly get to know about them in mediated forms. In a loop back through the previous section, we might note that reports of the performance of public services circulate primarily through mass media in a context of journalistic ambivalence (if not cynicism) about government (Phillis Report 2004). Media treatment of the reports of scrutiny agencies range from celebration of their 'watchdoggery' to cynicism about both government and producer interests (the 'burying of bad news'; the celebration of 'massaged' good news; or the effects of producer capture in producing obfuscatory comparisons).

The final paradox
Performance evaluation in a sceptical world

I have tried to indicate ways in which the contexts that have created the rise of performance evaluation systems as a key element of the co-ordination of public services also create the paradoxes that make performance evaluation the focus of different sorts of conflicts, competing objectives and political manoeuvring. Treating the contexts of public service reform as constitutive of these paradoxes suggests that they are unlikely to be resolved by technical, methodological or organisational innovations. I do not mean that performance evaluation systems cannot be improved in technical, methodological and organisational ways: clearly they have been, and will continue to be, improved by such innovations. But it is impossible for such innovations to resolve the paradoxes that emerged from the fundamentally political contexts involved in 'reinventing' or 'modernising' government and 'reforming' public services.

As a result, governments that have promoted a sceptical view of public services (insisting on the need for their transformation and subjection to new disciplines) will, in their turn, continue to be viewed sceptically by publics that mistrust politics and politicians (O'Neill 2002). The paradox of independence in which none of the legitimating claims about the independence of evaluators and evaluation can provide a secure and stable foundation in the face of less deferential and more fragmented publics means that performance evaluation systems cannot resolve the 'credibility' problem for governments. This is exacerbated by the mediated circulation of 'evidence' and its assessment in mass media that are predisposed towards 'market populism' (Frank 2001). Evaluation agencies have to deal with the paradoxes of their role as representatives of the public interest, imagined as the 'value for money' orientation of the taxpayer/consumer. Finally, the comparative-competitive model that has dominated the evaluation regime in the UK makes 'success' a highly valued construction with many different agents and agencies having a strong interest in being 'successful' (even as they know that being successful is a constructed or negotiated outcome, produced through particular criteria in specific social processes).

In the end, performance evaluation systems and processes cannot 'square the circle' of political and governmental paradoxes. They are compromised by the conditions of their invention. Apparatuses that promise transparency, accountability, evidence and the rational determination of the public interest have to operate in a sceptical world. They are located within political and cultural dynamics that have produced publics who want improved public services and who – unevenly and unpredictably – distrust the governmental machinery that tells them about improvement. That is the final – and possibly most fundamental – paradox of performance evaluation.

References

Audit Commission (2007) *Comprehensive Area Assessment*. London: Audit Commission.

Clarke, J. (2005a) 'Producing Transparency? Evaluation and the Governance of Public Services.' In G. Drewry, C. Greve and T. Tanquerel (eds) *Contracts, Performance Measurement and Accountability in the Public Sector*. Amsterdam: IOS Press.

Clarke, J. (2005b) 'Performing for the Public: Doubt, Desire and the Evaluation of Public Services.' In P. Du Gay (ed.) *The Values of Bureaucracy*. Oxford: Oxford University Press.

Clarke, J. (2006) 'Disorganizzare Il Publicco?' *La Rivista Delle Politiche Sociali 2* (April–June), 107–126.

Clarke, J. and Newman, J. (1997) *The Managerial State: Power, Politics and Ideology in the Remaking of Social Welfare*. London: Sage.

Clarke, J., Newman, J., Smith, N., Vidler, E. and Westmarland, L. (2007) *Creating Citizen-Consumers: Changing Publics and Changing Public Services*. London: Sage.

Cooper, D. (1998) *Governing out of Order: Space, Law and the Politics of Belonging*. London: Rivers Oram Press.

Cutler, T. and Waine, B. (1997) *Managing the Welfare State*. Oxford: Berg.

Davies, H., Nutley, S. M. and Smith, P. (eds) (2000) *What Works? Evidence-based Policy and Practice in Public Services*. Bristol: The Policy Press.

Davis, H., Downe, J. and Martin, S. J. (2001) *External Inspection of Local Government: Driving Improvement or Drowning in Detail*. York: Joseph Rowntree Foundation/York Publishing Services.

Day, P. and Klein, R. (1990) *Inspecting the Inspectorates*. York: Joseph Rowntree Foundation.

Downe, J. and Martin, S. J. (2007a) 'Inspecting for improvement? Emerging patterns of public service regulation in the UK.' *Environment and Planning C 25*, 410–422.

Downe, J. and Martin, S. J. (2007b) 'Regulation inside government: Processes and impacts of inspection of local public services.' *Policy and Politics 35*, 2, 215–232.

Frank, T. (2001) *One Market Under God: Extreme Capitalism, Market Populism and the End of Economic Democracy*. New York: Anchor Books.

Hackett, R. (2001) 'News Media and Civic Equality: Watch Dogs, Mad Dogs, or Lap Dogs?' In E. Broadbent (ed.) *Democratic Equality: What Went Wrong?* Toronto: University of Toronto Press.

Hansen, T. B. and Stepputat, F. (eds) (2001) *States of Imagination: Ethnographic Explorations of the Postcolonial State*. Durham, NC: Duke University Press.

Harper, R. (2000) 'The social Organization of the IMF's Mission Work: An Examination of International Auditing.' In M. Strathern (ed.) *Audit Cultures*. London: Routledge.

Hood, C. (1991) 'A public management for all seasons?' *Public Administration 69*, 1.

Hood, C., Scott, C., James, O., Jones, G. and Travers, T. (1998) *Regulation Inside Government: Waste-watchers, Quality Police and Sleaze Busters*. Oxford: Oxford University Press.

Humphrey, J. (2002) 'A scientific approach to politics? On the trail of the Audit Commission.' *Critical Perspectives on Accounting 13*, 39–62.

Larner, W. and Walters, W. (eds) (2004) *Global Governmentality*. London: Routledge.

Miller, D. (2005) 'What is Best "Value"? Bureaucracy, Virtualism and Local Governance.' In P. Du Gay (ed.) *The Values of Bureaucracy*. Oxford: Oxford University Press.

Needham, C. (2003) *Citizen-consumers: New Labour's Marketplace Democracy*. London: Catalyst Forum.

Office of the Deputy Prime Minister/HM Treasury (2005) *Securing Better Outcomes: Developing a New Performance Management Framework*. London: Office of the Deputy Prime Minister.

Office of Public Services Reform (OPSR) (2002) *Reforming Our Public Services*. London: OPSR.

Office of Public Services Reform (OPSR) (2003) *The Government's Policy on Inspection of Public Services*. London: OPSR.

O'Neill, O. (2002) *A Question of Trust (The BBC Reith Lectures 2002)*. Cambridge, Cambridge University Press.

Osborne, D. and Gaebler, T. (1992) *Reinventing Government: How the Entrepreneurial Spirit is Transforming the Public Sector*. Reading, MA: Addison-Wesley.

Paton, R. (2003) *Managing and Measuring Social Enterprises*. London: Sage.

Phillis Report (2004) *The Report of an Independent Review of Government Communications*. London: Cabinet Office.

Pollitt, C., Girre, X., Lonsdale, J., Mul, R., Summa, H. and Waerness, M. (1999) *Performance or Compliance? Performance Audit and Public Management in Five Countries*. Oxford: Oxford University Press.

Power, M. (1997) *The Audit Society*. Oxford: Oxford University Press.

Prince, M. (2001) 'How social is social policy? Fiscal and market discourse in North American welfare states.' *Social Policy and Administration 35*, 1, 2–13.

Schram, S. and Soss, J. (2002) 'Success Stories: Welfare Reform, Policy Discourse and the Politics of Research.' In S. Schram, *Praxis for the Poor*. New York: New York University Press.

Stein, J. (2001) *The Cult of Efficiency*. Toronto: House of Anansi Press.

Strathern, M. (2000) *Audit Cultures*. London: Routledge.

Trinder, L. and Reynolds, S. (eds) (2000) *Evidence-based Practice: A Critical Appraisal*. Oxford: Blackwell.

West, H. and Sanders, T. (eds) (2003) *Transparency and Conspiracy: Ethnographies of Suspicion in the New World Order*. Durham, NC: Duke University Press.

CHAPTER 9

The Future of Public Services Inspection

Howard Davis and Steve Martin

Introduction

As we noted in Chapter 1, in spite of the increasingly central role that inspection has played in the governance of local public services in the UK, there has been relatively little informed academic analysis of its development or its impact. In particular, as far as we know, there has not been any systematic attempt to assess the operation of inspection across different parts of the public services. The aim of this book has therefore been to bring together in one place authoritative and evidence-based analyses of the evolution, ethos and current operation of inspection on those local public services which have the most direct impact on service users and citizens.

The five chapters covering the inspection of the health service, social care, education and skills, local government and the criminal justice system provide insightful accounts of the changing nature and role of inspection in each of these sectors. We hope that they will help to advance both academic and policy debates about the costs and benefits of public services inspection as it is currently preached and practised in the UK. In addition, we wanted this book to provide a basis for looking across these traditional public service 'silos' in order to identify common themes and differences in the way in which inspection has developed. As well as looking at past developments and the current operation of inspection, we hoped to be able to draw some conclusions about the future dilemmas, challenges and choices that await policymakers and inspectors. Chapters 7 and 8 by Steve Bundred and Clive Grace and by John Clarke identify some of the important generic issues and challenges which apply to almost all parts of the public service. In this final chapter we want to pull together and reflect on the key conclusions to emerge from these and the five chapters focused on individual sectors.

After ten years of increasingly intensive inspection of public services, now seems a good time to try to take stock of what has (and has not) been achieved. The speed at which inspection frameworks continue to change and develop (an issue that we will return to shortly) means that some of the details about how individual inspection regimes operate may well have changed yet again even by the time this book is published. But that is not the point. Its purpose has been to take a slightly longer and wider view, identifying similarities and differences between different public services and continuity and change over time. So we start by identifying common themes and messages to emerge from the seven contributions to this volume. We then review the evidence they provide about the impacts of public services inspection. Finally, we consider the implications for the future development of inspection.

Common themes

The chapters highlight a number of important recurring themes that apply right across key local public services. Five of these seem to us to be of particular importance in attempting to analyse the changing character of inspection:

- inspection for improvement
- convergence
- from services to organisations to area-based inspection
- the pace of change
- devolution and divergence.

Inspection for improvement

All of the chapters highlight the unprecedented focus that there has been on public services improvement in the UK over the last decade, and they demonstrate the degree to which policymakers have come to rely on inspection as one of the principal means of 'driving' improvement. The current faith in inspection is without precedent in the UK and without parallel anywhere else in the world. International observers are frequently intrigued, though at times somewhat baffled, by our acceptance of and apparent addiction to externally imposed performance frameworks. Seen from an international perspective, the UK is a fascinating, though slightly bizarre, experiment in public services reform which is testing the effectiveness of top-down, centrally driven initiatives to the outer limits.

Convergence

Second, all of the chapters in this book show how in the last ten years there has been a very significant shift in the nature of inspection. A decade ago different parts of the public sector were subject to quite different inspection arrangements – and in some cases none at all. Regulation of services really was 'silo based' and often still rooted in professional assumptions and norms. Many of the inspection frameworks were what McGarvey and Stoker (1999) call 'collegial/emancipatory' regimes and retained a strong emphasis on self-evaluation and self-regulation. This is no longer the case. Over the last decade the same theory of improvement has been applied to schools, hospitals, social care, housing, the police, the courts, the probation service, fire and rescue and a range of other services. This has had much to do with the Labour government's determination to drive up standards and to do so as rapidly as possible. As a result inspection has focused not just on current performance but also on prospects for improvement, and approaches to inspection right across the public services have drawn on the same core set of assumptions about what is needed to achieve and sustain this.

There has then been a marked shift towards an overtly 'managerial' approach. Effective managerial leadership, corporate capacity and robust performance management have been seen as the key ingredients of good performance in all services. The assumption has been that this same toolkit of core management techniques works equally well in all service settings. The various local inspectorates have therefore increasingly adopted the same inspection methodology. Not surprisingly, this has posed significant new challenges – for staff who are managing 'frontline' services; for managers and local politicians charged with overseeing services; and for the inspectors who have often found themselves scrutinising performance in service areas outside of their own professional training and expertise.

From services to organisations to area-based inspection

A third key message to emerge from this book is that the focus of inspection has changed fundamentally. As well as being concerned with the performance of individual services, inspectors now invest considerable time and resources in assessing an organisation's culture and capacity.

The emergence of a hegemonic theory of improvement and the associated convergence in inspection methods has facilitated the development of a more 'joined up' approach to inspection across the public sector as a whole. This has in turn prepared the way for a move 'up' from the inspection of individual services and public service organisations (councils, hospitals, schools, etc.) to an area-based inspection framework such as Comprehensive Area Assessments. It is consistent with the emphasis on more joined up, seamless, service delivery and better partnership working through the creation of Local Strategic Partnerships, Local Area Agreements and Multi-Area Agreements in England, the duty of community planning in Scotland, and the development of Local Service Boards and Local Service Agreements in Wales.

The pace of change

A fourth important theme highlighted by previous chapters is the underlying sense of urgency and the pace of change in inspection frameworks. The government is, it seems, unable to resist the temptation constantly to tinker with the institutional infrastructure of inspection – creating, merging and then often abolishing inspectorates with almost mind-numbing rapidity. Some inspectorates have only lasted a year or two. Others have seen significant and repeated changes in their identities, roles, remits and responsibilities. Most have therefore felt the need to refine and redefine their mission and methods. As many of the chapters in this book illustrate, no sooner has one inspection framework been agreed and 'rolled out' than government departments and the inspectorates have begun work on the development of its successor. In the world of public services inspection constant change really does seem to be here to stay.

There is a positive side to all of this upheaval. Many of the changes have been made in an attempt to respond to criticisms from inspected bodies. Examples include ongoing attempts to develop 'joined up' inspection and to reduce the 'burden' of inspection by developing more 'proportionate' or 'risk-based' approaches. Moreover, there are some good reasons for moving the goalposts fairly regularly. It reduces the opportunities for gaming by the inspected bodies and helps to guard against complacency by regularly raising the performance bar. But keeping practitioners 'on the hop' also poses some significant difficulties. It undoubtedly distracts from the 'real' job of frontline delivery and it often corrodes staff morale. Local service providers have to set aside significant amounts of staff resources just to keep abreast of the latest government thinking and to respond to the latest initiatives. Many have had to create new posts for dedicated staff whose job is simply to prepare their organisations for inspections, providing the data requested by inspectors, briefing potential interviewees, managing site visits and negotiating with the inspectors about their judgements and the contents of their reports. Moreover, many service providers have of course lost some of their more experienced professionals to the swelling ranks of the inspectors.

But the cost of inspection is not just to be counted in terms of staff who might otherwise have been gainfully employed in delivering services 'on the ground'. Centrally imposed targets, performance measures and inspection frameworks have rendered local authority chief executives, chief constables and health service managers more accountable 'upwards' to government departments (be they in London, Edinburgh or Cardiff), but have made it more difficult for local service providers to tailor what they do to local needs, preferences and priorities. Inspection has also encouraged a compliance mentality. Professionals have felt increasingly distrusted and deprived of discretion, and resigned themselves to simply 'jumping through the requisite hoops' or 'ticking the boxes'. Treating local service providers and their staff as the front end of a centrally driven 'delivery chain' clearly runs the risk that they lack the incentive, and eventually lose the appetite, to think creatively about how best to meet the needs of their particular localities and client groups.

Devolution and divergence

Finally, the accounts provided by the previous chapters suggest growing evidence that at the same time as models of improvement and approaches to inspection in different services have been converging, the creation of devolved administrations in Scotland and Wales has led to the emergence of distinctive strategies for public services reform which have in turn begun to produce divergent approaches to the inspection of local public services (Downe et al. 2007). Potentially the UK is therefore not just a testing ground for public services inspection but also a laboratory in which rather different approaches to inspection are being experimented with. This opens up the possibility for learning between the different parts of the UK and the possibility that Northern Ireland, Scotland and Wales may begin to compare experiences with other smaller European countries with which in some senses at least they have more in common than they do with England.

The impacts of inspection

Fascinating though the changing character of public services inspection is – and what it tells us about the overall strategy for public services reform – the real question, for policymakers at least, is whether it has made any difference. What then do we really know about the impacts of public services inspection? It really ought to be possible after ten years of more or less universal inspection of public services in the UK to draw some reasonably robust conclusions about what it has and has not achieved. Chapters 2 to 6 have all attempted to bring together the evidence relating to the sectors which they focus on. But all of the authors conclude that evaluating the impact of inspection is extremely difficult. The claims and counterclaims made by advocates and critics of the current approach to inspection have not, on the whole, been subject to rigorous academic scrutiny. The UK government, which has trumpeted its commitment to 'evidence-based policy making' and actively supported evaluations of almost all of its key policies and initiatives, has proved remarkably shy about commissioning research on the impacts of inspection. There has been internal debate within the inspectorates about their effectiveness. But understandably, given the febrile environment and highly political environment in which they operate, there is an apparent reluctance to bring the discussion out into the open. This has made for a somewhat muted and often rather ill-informed public debate, much of which has been based on anecdotal accounts rather than empirical analysis. There are two key criteria in terms of which the impact of inspection should be judged: has it supported performance improvement and/or has it secured greater public accountability?

Supporting improvement

Since the time when inspection first came to the fore, there have been significant improvements in management systems and practices in many public services and a discernible improvement in 'corporate capacity', particularly in some of the worst performing organisations. There was, for example, a steady increase in the numbers of councils in England rated in the top two categories in the Comprehensive Performance Assessment (CPA) in spite of a significant tightening up of the criteria (Audit Commission 2007a). The inspectors have also reported improvements in the ways in which local authorities manage their resources (Audit Commission 2008).

Patterns of improvement in outcomes (as opposed to internal systems and practices) are more complex and there have been differences between different service areas and between different organisations. But here too there is evidence – from inspections, statutory performance indicators and public satisfaction surveys – which suggests that there have been some impressive achievements (Martin 2008). Analyses by the Commission for Social Care Inspection and Her Majesty's Chief Inspector of Education, Children's Services and Skills, for example, have concluded that overall there has been significant improvement in both children's services and adult social services in recent years, particularly in the social services departments that have started from the lowest base in terms of performance. There have also been improvements in some, though not all, of the indicators of educational attainment. In health some of the government's key measures, such as waiting times, have improved, particularly in England.

Of course, as Jane Martin explains in Chapter 4, it is impossible to establish a precise causal link between inspection and these improvements. Performance is determined by a complex interplay of a range of different factors which include the socio-economic and demographic characteristics of an area, organisational cultures and individual actions. But it does seem clear that inspection has been a contributory factor. Grace and Martin (2008) report that improvement in local government performance has been facilitated by the combination of real terms increases in funding and a determined drive by central government, plus the support and challenge provided by the inspectorates and improvement agencies. This has, they suggest, resulted in a greater willingness and capacity on the part of many councils to take responsibility for their own improvement and an increased emphasis on users' needs.

Several of the contributions to this book also point to clear evidence of the ways in which inspection can encourage performance improvement. In Chapter 2 James Downe highlights the findings of surveys of local authority officers which show that they regard inspection, and in particular CPA, as one of the most important 'drivers' of improvement in their organisations. In Chapter 5 Kieran Walshe concludes that the Commission for Health Improvement's clinical governance process played an important role, alongside other reforms, in changing the priorities and improving the performance of NHS organisations. In Chapter 6 John Raine reports that the work of Her Majesty's Inspectorate of Constabulary has led to improvements in managerial practices in the police and improved performance as measured by detection rates and crime reduction figures. He also credits Her Majesty's Inspectorate of Court Administration with improving court procedures and accommodation and reducing variability in practices. He concludes that Her Majesty's Crown Prosecution Service Inspectorate has led to improvements in and standardisation of managerial processes and performance efficiency across the country.

Securing accountability

The second question concerning impact is whether inspection has enhanced accountability to the citizens and service users. Here its achievements seem less impressive. With the notable exception of school league tables, the public has, on the whole, shown precious little interest in inspection reports or star ratings. As noted above, public services managers report that while inspection has increased their accountability to central government it has done very little to enhance local accountability mechanisms. If inspection has had any effect at all on the relationship with the public, the signs are that it may have dented confidence. In spite of better performance in terms of CPA scores, performance indicators, and user satisfaction with services, the public's rating of councils' overall performance has declined in recent years, and a majority of citizens are pessimistic about the prospects for future improvement in services. In 2007 fewer than a quarter believed that the NHS would improve or that crime rates were likely to come down, and fewer than a third thought the quality of education, public transport, opportunities for young people or skills training would get better (Ipsos MORI 2007). This evidence is consistent with O'Neill's (2002) thesis that while inspection and audit agencies purport to serve citizens and service users by providing them with necessary information about performance, in fact they erode trust between professionals and the public.

The future

Is inspection improving?

In our view the frameworks for local inspection have improved over the last ten years. Tangible improvements in many services suggest that underperforming hospitals, police services, schools, councils and prisons benefited from robust external challenge. Inspection raised awareness of weaknesses and the threat of intervention motivated public service providers to tackle deficiencies. On the whole it made sense for inspection to focus on the leadership of the whole organisation. As noted above, there has also been considerable progress towards achieving a more 'joined up' approach across all public services. The development of less 'silo based' inspection is consistent with the government's attempts to encourage better partnership working at local level. The reduction in the number of local inspectorates can be seen as a logical next step along this path, and there is a good case for trying to move up from a focus on the performance of individual organisations to more holistic, area-based assessments. The increasing emphasis on 'strategic' regulation and more carefully targeted inspection is also an improvement on the one-size-fits-all, blanket coverage of recent years. There are though a number of challenges and tensions which have not yet been resolved, and it is to these that we turn in the closing section of this book.

Inspection and scrutiny

First, the links between external inspection and other accountability mechanisms have still not been properly thought through or sufficiently well developed. There is a multitude of often unrelated plans, audits, inspections, local scrutiny bodies, complaints systems, standards bodies and 'ombudsmen' which continue to operate largely in isolation. Thus an independent review of the future of local public services in Wales, under the chairmanship of Sir Jeremy Beecham, concluded in 2006 that accountability arrangements were unnecessarily complex and need to be rationalised (Welsh Assembly Government, 2006). An independent review of external scrutiny in Scotland in 2007 reached similar conclusions, noting that the 'accountability landscape' has become cluttered with 'large numbers of different players with the ability and right to both direct and create new scrutiny' and that this is both costly and makes 'joint working on cross-cutting and complex issues more difficult to organise effectively' (Scottish Government 2007, summary).

Mission creep and multiple identities

As several of the earlier chapters have illustrated, the remit of inspection has increased enormously in recent years. Inspectors no longer simply check on current performance, they now also make judgements about prospects for future improvement based on assessments of its leadership and managerial capacity. In the process they have begun (implicitly at least) to encourage the development of particular cultural norms, organisational characteristics and managerial practices. As James Downe and John Clarke (in Chapters 2 and 8) both note, the 'watchdogs' are now becoming 'guide dogs'. This is reflected by the Audit Commission's description of its roles which features on the inside front cover of its reports. This explains that the Commission is now:

- 'an independent body responsible for ensuring that public money is spent economically, efficiently and effectively, to achieve high-quality local services for the public'

- 'an independent watchdog' providing 'important information on the quality of public services'

- 'a driving force for improvement' providing 'practical recommendations and spread[ing] best practice'

- 'an independent auditor' ensuring 'that public services are good value for money and that public money is properly spent'.

A decade ago the claims made by inspectorates were much more modest. As recently as 2003 (in the course of research we were undertaking on the inspection of local government – see Davis, Downe and Martin 2004) senior inspectors insisted that they were responsible for inspecting services, not organisations. They were adamant that their role was to be 'an inspection service not an improvement service'. They did not therefore seek to disseminate 'good practice' or dispense advice on how inspected bodies might improve. As one of us has argued elsewhere (Martin 2004), this clear demarcation has strong attractions and some observers see the recent expansion of the inspectors' role as unwelcome 'mission creep'. It is not at all clear that the inspectorates really can be both an 'independent watchdog' and a driving force for improvement which provides practical recommendations on how to improve. Agents of improvement need to be close to and trusted by the organisations that they are advising. In contrast, independent regulators need to maintain some level of relational distance if they are to retain their credibility. In our view, inspectorates need to guard their independence above all else and the best way to do this is to hold inspected bodies to account for improving but to leave the job of giving practical advice and disseminating good practice to the improvement agencies, professional networks, leadership centres and multitude of capacity building programmes.

Whose improvement?

Performance in the public sector is multidimensional and different stakeholders will value different kinds of improvement. Service users, for example, may place a premium on the quality of local services, while taxpayers are likely to weight value for money highly. Moreover, definitions of performance change over time. For several years the main focus of inspection has been on service standards. Now though, use of resources is one of the key criteria against which a council's performance is judged by the Audit Commission. Moreover, thinking about what constitutes 'resources' is also developing. Two or three years ago very few councils, schools or hospitals would have considered their 'carbon footprint' to be an important performance measure, but indicators of environmental impact are now becoming important. Similarly, area-based outcomes have moved rapidly up the agenda. As Bundred and Grace argue in Chapter 7, the inspectorates are increasingly seeking to put citizen and service user perspectives at the heart of inspection frameworks.

So it is important that priorities for and definitions of improvement are kept under review and remain up to date. Yet there is a danger that, for understandable reasons, inspection will continue to focus on those aspects of performance that are easiest to measure, rather than on those which are most important. This exacerbates the 'disconnect' between the managerial ethos and language of inspection and the 'bread and butter' issues that matter most to voters and therefore to local politicians. National performance frameworks and incentives can all too easily ride roughshod over local priorities. To date local and central government have made little progress in convincing a sceptical public of the desirability of some of the major changes in the delivery of services which they wish to pursue – including, for example, the closure of small local hospitals and rural schools and moves to fortnightly refuse collections. Perhaps it is no wonder then that some local politicians regard inspection as a sideshow, and public confidence has not increased in spite of the demonstrable improvement in services.

The 'place shaping' agenda advocated by the Lyons Inquiry into the future form and function of local government, and endorsed in the 2006 Local Government White Paper, throws the potential conflict between national priorities and what matters locally and 'politically' into even sharper relief. It is difficult to see how a standard set of performance criteria, of the kind which have been used in inspection frameworks over the last decade, will survive as localities are increasingly encouraged to shape their own priorities and one size cannot therefore any longer fit them all.

Beyond competence

Probably the single most important question for the future of inspection is whether it will be able to support the kinds of improvements that will matter most over the next decade. Inspection has undoubtedly strengthened managerial capacity and encouraged the development of a more performance oriented culture in UK public services. With this has come a much stronger focus than ever before on the need for improvements, particularly in those services and organisations that have been deemed to be the worst performers. Even its harshest critics would probably accept that inspection has provided senior officers, service managers and local politicians with more comprehensive data than they have ever had before, making it easier for them to identify failing services and more difficult to ignore them.

But the inspection frameworks of the last ten years have been focused on quite narrowly defined performance criteria. Inspectors have often seemed concerned as much with managerial processes as with service outcomes. As noted above, until fairly recently they have also been more interested in service quality than public sector productivity. The main imperative has been to raise the performance of failing services rather than to help those occupying the upper echelons of performance league tables to do even better. CPA and other performance frameworks have therefore rewarded compliance with existing models of good managerial practice, rather than seeking to encourage new approaches. As Swann *et al.* argue:

> Too often *improvement* is not seen as being about improving the life chances of individuals and communities or about building a stronger democracy. Instead *Improvement* (note the capital 'I') is seen as being about managerial compliance with an externally imposed assessment process. (Swann *et al.* 2005, p.3)

As a result, 'much of the current improvement apparatus is effective at supporting councils to become competent organisations' but it is not designed to move them 'beyond competence' into a position where they are able to develop innovative approaches with the potential to transform services (Swann *et al.* 2005, p.9).

Achieving 'competence' has been no mean feat for some of the services and organisations that were deemed to be failing. But whilst this may be enough to move an organisation from 'awful to adequate', it is probably not sufficient to enable it to meet the challenges that lie ahead. After several years of large, real-terms increases in public spending, budgets are now much tighter and yet public expectations continue to escalate. Doing the same thing a little better probably will not produce the improvements in performance and efficiency that are needed. Service providers are going to have to do different things – to develop new services, change delivery processes and find new ways of working across organisational boundaries (Audit Commission 2007b). Creating conditions that encourage innovation and transformational change, rather than incremental improvements, will have important implications for inspection. As Mulgan notes:

> Despite the rhetorical lip service paid to innovation, no government has anything remotely comparable to the armies of civil servants employed to count things, to inspect and to monitor or, for that matter, to support tech-nological research and development. (Mulgan 2007, p.4)

Whether the inspectorates will be able to identify, support and reward the kind of leadership that is needed to achieve transformational change is unclear. Innovation is often risky. Some attempts to develop new approaches will fail and inspection will therefore need to make allowances for this and for short-term dips in performance that accompany even some of the most successful innovations as staff adjust to new ways of working.

Aligning the practice of public services inspection with the principles of reform

Shortly before he stepped down as Prime Minister, Tony Blair reaffirmed his commitment to four 'principles of public service reform':

1.   Empowering the user.

2.   Opening up the service to a diversity of supply.

3. Making sure we get to the hardest to reach.

4. Allowing the workforce the innovation and creativity that they want and need in order to create a service 'that is genuinely fair to all, but personal to each' (Blair 2007, p.4).

His Strategy Unit published a discussion paper setting out 'the government's approach to public service reform' (Cabinet Office 2006). Like his predecessor, Prime Minister Gordon Brown has made it clear that he believes there is a need to push public services reform much further. He has emphasised the need to tackle 'inequalities in aspiration and capability' and promote the personalisation of services (Brown 2007), and it seems likely that he will therefore be guided by the same broad principles as Blair.

A genuine restructuring of public services around these (or a similar set of) principles would have major implications for inspection. If users were to be empowered and more willing to be engaged in monitoring services and outcomes, this could lead to a reduced role for inspection. 'Bottom-up' pressure from service users and citizens might be seen as replacing 'top-down' inspection and performance frameworks. Equally though, inspection could be seen as having a key role to play in empowering users. It could report on users' views of performance and provide the public with comparative analyses of outcomes over time to help them make informed choices and decisions. Inspection could help to promote the needs of 'hard to reach' groups by paying particular attention to their views and interests.

Opening up services to a diversity of supply would imply a role for regulators which is more akin to that of the regulators of privatised utilities – water, electricity and gas suppliers, the train operating companies, and so forth. As we noted in Chapter 1, this implies establishing the rules by which suppliers operate and seeking to increase competition by opening up markets to new providers. As we also explained in Chapter 1, some local inspectorates already see their role partly in these terms. However, the increasing emphasis on involving the private and third sectors in public service provision (Kelly 2007) could take inspectorates much deeper into the territory of actively creating conditions which encourage new entrants to markets.

For the reasons that we explored earlier in this chapter, in our view, the fourth of the prime ministerial principles – allowing staff to be more creative and innovative – would mean that local service providers would have to be granted more freedom than current inspection frameworks give. In short, central government would have to be willing to 'let go' in a way in which it has not so far felt able to do, and local service providers would need to take more responsibility for ensuring their own improvement. This would undoubtedly be seen by some as a risky strategy. But it is not perhaps such a distant prospect as it once seemed. In local government, for example, there is now much greater ownership of the improvement agenda at local level than there was even two or three years ago, and the national representative bodies (such as the Local Government Association) and political parties are less willing to tolerate or excuse poor performance by councils than they were in the past.

In recent years it has been central government that has set the targets and the local inspectorates have checked whether these have been met. Agencies such as the Local Government Leadership Centre and Improvement and Development Agency have been charged with helping councils to develop the capacity to rise to the challenges set for them by central government. In theory there is no reason why the sector itself cannot take much more responsibility for setting the standards and reviewing progress against them. The 2006 Local Government White Paper signalled the government's intention to give more space for self-regulation of this kind, and it might be argued that improvements in 'corporate capacity' make it easier for ministers to trust councils. The same logic potentially applies to other public services. In February 2007, for instance, the Fire Minister Angela Smith announced:

> The fire and rescue service has been undergoing a significant change programme over the past few years so that it is better equipped to meet the challenges of today's world. The way in which Government engages with the service has also been subject to review. As a consequence the role and function of HM Fire Service Inspectorate has changed and it no longer undertakes its original core role of inspecting all fire and rescue services in England. We have, therefore, decided that it is no longer appropriate to retain the Inspectorate in its current form and that a new professional advisory unit would be better placed to provide independent support to Ministers and officials. (Smith 2007)

The primary responsibility of this new unit will, she said, be to provide ministers and officials 'with direct access to a source of authoritative independent professional advice on matters of structure, organisation, performance and future development of fire and rescue business' (Smith 2007).

It is possible that some other local inspectorates could also be called upon to focus less on inspection and more on offering advice on policy and practice.

Beyond these possible implications of the current administration's principles of public services reform there is, of course, the possibility that a change of government might take public services reform in an altogether different direction which lead to a rethinking of the role of inspection. The Scottish Nationalists and Plaid Cymru – both now in government for the first time – are likely to want to carve out more distinctively Scottish and Welsh approaches to the regulation of public services. Under David Cameron, the Conservatives have spoken of the arrival of a 'post-bureaucratic age' in which power should be returned to 'frontline' professionals – teachers, clinicians, social workers, etc. – and central government needs to embrace a far more localist agenda. On the face of it a change of UK government could therefore signal a reduced role for 'top down' inspection driven by the centre.

Whatever the future holds, it is clear that a combination of tighter resources and rising expectations – on the part of both the public and politicians – will continue to drive demands for better, more personalised, more responsive, more efficient, and more cost-effective public services. This may throw some of the tensions between national and local priorities into even sharper relief. But the inspectorates have demonstrated a remarkable capacity to adapt and respond to changing government priorities, and in our view the smart money is on continued refining and fine tuning of inspection of public services, rather than its wholesale abandonment.

References

Audit Commission (2007a) *Comprehensive Performance Assessment: The Harder Test – Scores and Analysis of Performance in Single Tier and County Councils 2006.* London: Audit Commission.

Audit Commission (2007b) *Seeing the Light: Innovation in Local Public Services.* London: Audit Commission.

Audit Commission (2008) *Use of Resources – Single Tier, County Council and District Council Scores for 2007.* London: Audit Commission.

Blair, T. (2007) *Speech to the Public Services Reform Conference,* 27 March. Available at http://www.number10.gov.uk/output/page 11358.asp., accessed 2 July 2008.

Brown, G. (2007) *Speech at the University of Greenwich,* 31 October. Available at http://www.number10.gov.uk/output/page 13675.asp, accessed 2 July 2008.

Cabinet Office (2006) *The UK Government's Approach to Public Service Reform: A Discussion Paper.* London: The Stationery Office.

Davis, H., Downe, J. and Martin, S. (2004) *The Changing Role of Audit Commission Inspection of Local Government*. York: York Publishing Services for the Joseph Rowntree Foundation.

Downe, J., Grace, C., Martin, S. J. and Nutley, S. M. (2007) 'Performance Regimes in England, Scotland and Wales.' In C. Grace (ed.) *Comparing for Improvement*. Solace Foundation Imprint: London.

Grace, C. and Martin, S.J. (2008) *Getting Better All the Time: An Independent Assessment of Local Government and Its Future Prospects*. London: IDeA.

Ipsos MORI (2007) *The Ipsos MORI Delivery Index*. London: Ipsos MORI.

Kelly, J. (2007) 'Reforming public services in the UK: Bringing in the third sector.' *Public Administration 85*, 4, 1003–1022.

McGarvey, N. and Stoker, G. (1999) *Intervention, Inspection, Regulation and Accountability in Local Government: Interim Literature Review*. London: Department of the Environment, Transport and the Regions.

Martin, S. J. (2004) 'The changing face of public inspection.' *Public Money and Management 24*, 1, 3–5.

Martin, S. J. (2008) *The State of Local Services: Performance Improvement in Local Government*. London: Department for Communities and Local Government.

Mulgan, G. (2007) *Ready or not? Taking Innovation in the Public Sector Seriously*. London: National Endowment for Science, Technology and the Arts.

O'Neill, O. (2002) *A Question of Trust: The BBC Reith Lectures 2002*. Cambridge: Cambridge University Press.

Scottish Government (2007) *The Crerar Review: The Report of the Independent Review of Regulation, Inspection, Audit and Complaints Handling of Public Services in Scotland*. Edinburgh: Scottish Government.

Smith, A. (2007) *Written Ministerial Statement,* Column 41WS, 8 February. London: House of Commons.

Swann, P., Davis, H., Kelleher, J., Ritters, K., Sullivan, F. and Hobson, M. (2005) *Beyond Competence: Driving Local Government Improvement*. London: Local Government Association.

Welsh Assembly Government (WAG) (2006) *Beyond Boundaries: Citizen-centred Local Services for Wales*. Cardiff: Welsh Assembly Government.

The Editors

Howard Davis is Acting Director of the Local Government Centre, Warwick Business School. He has for many years been centrally involved in projects advising on and/or evaluating the modernisation and improvement of local government – commissioned by both national and local government.

He co-led the first quinquennial review of the Improvement and Development Agency for Local Government and an impact assessment of local government's Performance Partnership. He also led the team which evaluated the Innovation Forum and the Shared Priorities for Public Services on behalf of the then ODPM and the Local Government Association and was part of the team which evaluated Freedoms and Flexibilities for local government on behalf of the DCLG.

In addition Howard has over a decade of experience of international working with particular reference to improving the delivery of local and public services in Central and Eastern Europe.

Steve Martin is Professor of Public Policy and Management at Cardiff Business School and the Director of Cardiff University's Centre for Local and Regional Government Research. Over the last 20 years Steve has directed numerous evaluations of public services reforms funded by UK government departments, the European Commission, the Economic and Social Research Council, the Joseph Rowntree and Nuffield Foundations and a wide range of other agencies. He has written widely on public services reform and policy evaluation and is the author of numerous reports commissioned by governments and other agencies.

Steve is a member of the board of directors of the Improvement and Development Agency and of the New Local Government Network. He advised Sir Michael Lyons' inquiry into the form and functions of local government and served as the academic adviser to the review of local public services in Wales conducted by Sir Jeremy Beecham in 2005/2006.

The Contributors

Steve Bundred is Chief Executive of the Audit Commission. Prior to taking up this appointment he was the Executive Director of the Improvement and Development Agency and Chief Executive of the London Borough of Camden.

John Clarke is Professor of Social Policy at the Open University. He is a leading researcher and commentator on the politics and ideologies of welfare and the implications and impacts of managerialism.

James Downe is Senior Research Fellow at the Centre for Local and Regional Government Research at Cardiff University. He has previously held academic posts at Warwick and Plymouth Universities and is an expert in local government policy.

Clive Grace is an Honorary Research Fellow at the Centre for Local and Regional Government Research at Cardiff University. He is the Chair of: Solace Foundation Imprint; the Local Better Regulation Office; the Research Councils' Shared Services Centre Ltd; Supporta plc; and of the International Panel of CIPFA.

Chris Johns is Senior Lecturer in the Centre for Interprofessional Studies at University of Wales Institute, Cardiff and an acknowledged expert in social care policy.

David Lock is a Senior Lecturer and the Programme Director of the MSc in Interprofessional Studies and the Regulation of Care Services Award at University of Wales Institute, Cardiff. His research is focused on the evaluation and regulation of social and health care.

Jane Martin is Director of Policy and Engagement at the Local Better Regulation Office. Prior to this she worked as a Senior Research Fellow at Warwick Business School and between 2003 and 2006 she was the first director of the Centre for Public Scrutiny.

John W. Raine is Professor of Management in Criminal Justice at the Institute of Local Government Studies, the University of Birmingham. He has conducted research and taught in the field of criminal justice for 25years and has been an adviser for a range of government departments and agencies in the UK and Europe.

Kieran Walshe is Co-Director of the Centre for Public Policy and Management and Professor of Health Policy and Management at Manchester Business School. His previous posts include spells working at the University of Birmingham, the University of California at Berkeley, and the King's Fund.

Subject Index

Author Index